Many thanks to my supportive and loving husband Charles who helped make this book a reality. I am eternally grateful for your selfless vision to help other parents who share our journey and your unending love and dedication to our son.

I am forever grateful to my best friend Crissa for the many hours of listening, brainstorming, and most of all encouragement.

My heartfelt appreciation goes out to all of my family for the love and support you continue to offer.

Most of all I am thankful for my amazing son Jacob to whom this book is dedicated. Without you I would have never been given this view of life or opportunity to help others find the peace and joy we have found by learning how to adapt to our A-typical journey.

No More Chasing "Normal"

The Emotional Survival Guide for Parents of Children with Autism, Down Syndrome, and All Other Disabilities.

"1 in every 6 children in the US has one or more developmental disabilities..." Center for Disease Control, 2016

Millions of Parents in the United States have a child that is diagnosed with some form of disability. The presence of a disability changes the course of their lives, hopes, and dreams. They find themselves suddenly surrounded by everyone else living their "normal" lives leaving them to wonder, where do we fit or where will my child fit? They experience a form of grief but are often unprepared because of a lack of information available on the topic. This book provides an in-depth look at the emotional impacts faced by these parents. This is the stuff your research doesn't tell you.

Loresa Stansell, MA, LPC, NCC

1434

Printed and bound in the USA.

ISBN-13:978-1974060443

ISBN-10:1974060446

Library of Congress Control Number: 2017912897

CreateSpace Independent Publishing Platform, North Charleston, SC.

Table of Contents

Introduction

It is my belief that everyone living outside of the expected norms of their society experiences some form of grief. If you never marry, you are living outside the expected norm of our society. If you are married but childless, again you defy the norm or expected life script. Basically, if you find yourself in any category that does not fall within the "normal" expected life script, you know it! You are reminded of your differences every time you interact with the majority in your society who has the "normal" expected life script.

It is difficult, at best, to describe the experience of learning that your child has a disability. A developmental disability marks the loss of "normal" that we all expect to have when we have children. Our expectations, hopes, and dreams are shattered, or at least shaken to the core. The fear, uncertainty, guilt, injustice, disbelief, overwhelming love, pride, need to protect, determination, sorrow, and shame for feeling grief are all interwoven to form a blanket of emotions that wrap around every aspect of your life in one swift motion. This emotional turmoil is the start of the rollercoaster ride I call A-typical Cyclic Grief.

In this book, we will be addressing this specific type of grief experienced by parents raising a child, or adult child that has one or more developmental disabilities.

The loss of "normal" impacts your sense of belonging, connectedness, worth, and familiarity. Everything you expected and anticipated as a parent has changed. The A-typical Cyclic Grief Model (diagram included on the next page) describes the various stages of grief or emotional responses to the loss of "normal" and gives us a visual of the cycle that repeats over the lifespan. It is a snapshot of the common emotional reactions we face as parents of a child or children with a disability.

The stages for the model began to come into view as I watched and listened to parents of children with disabilities through the years. Raising a son with autism, gave me firsthand experience of this type of grief, leading me to countless hours of research on the topic. I have also had the privilege of working with college students with disabilities, volunteering as a parent trainer with NAMI (National Alliance for Mental Illness), working with parents in a local autism support group, and helping parents of children with a variety of disabilities in my counseling practice.

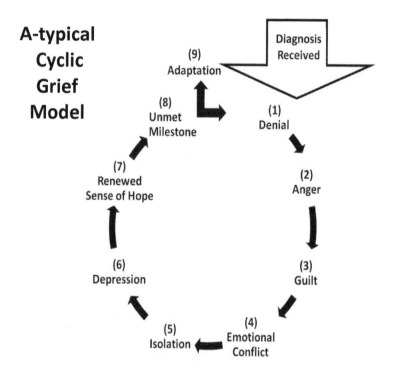

As you can see, the model is a loop with only one arrow exiting or breaking the cycle. The loop is significant because I believe we continue to cycle through the grief stages as long as we try to accept a final outcome, continue to chase "normal", or try to get back what was lost. Each time we encounter a new unmet milestone, it signifies another loss which launches us back into the cycle of grief.

In 1969, Elisabeth Kubler Ross described the grief she observed in patients faced with death or the loss of a loved one. The stages are widely familiar today and are described as Denial, Anger, Bargaining, Depression, and Acceptance. She explained that the stages do not necessarily occur in an exact order and that people can commonly move between the stages and possibly repeat the stages several times throughout the grief process. Her model became the standard to understand grief, when people experienced grief due to death.

When someone has died, the grief is very real and very painful to get through. It is not uncommon for people who have lost a loved one to keep their rooms intact or their belongings untouched.

When I am working with clients that have lost a loved one, typically, they will talk about keeping everything the same. Sometimes months or years will pass before they are able to move their loved one's items out of the closet or go through personal belongings. They talk about the nostalgia of being able to hear their loved one's voice on saved phone messages and seeing their slippers by the door.

Sameness represents a source of comfort and normalcy. These behaviors make people feel like the person is still with them, close to them. They are tip-toeing towards acceptance because they are not quite ready to say goodbye yet psychologically.

Because death is a final outcome and unchanging, people eventually come to realize that their loved one is gone and nothing they do will change the circumstance. In time, they come to accept the person's absence and learn how to go on without them. The loss is always there, but death is final and unchanging.

This fact eventually leads people to the acceptance stage of grief. Of course they cycle through painful emotions during the grief process, but at some point, the finality of the death is accepted. In contrast, A-typical Cyclic Grief has no acceptance stage because nothing final has occurred. Even though it may appear final on the surface, nothing could be farther from the truth.

Think about it. Our children will constantly change and grow, which makes it difficult, if not virtually impossible, to know what to accept. For many, it is difficult to know how our children will respond to treatment and interventions. Therefore, we move through the cycles over and over again. It is like being stuck on an emotional treadmill. That is one of the significant differences in understanding A-typical Cyclic Grief and what makes it unique from other types of grief. It can be a yoyo effect. If our children are making developmental or academic gains, our grief is replaced by hope that they will be okay, maybe close to "normal."

When a milestone is missed or progression stops or slows, we experience grief all over again. The final stage of ACG is Adapting not Acceptance. Learning how to get off the treadmill and adapt to your new normal rather than chasing the lost "normal" is critical! Understanding the ebb and flow instead of looking for a final mark or destination is a key component to adapting.

Another difference in the type of grief we experience is the lack of support or understanding offered by others. A-typical Cyclic Grief (ACG) usually does not cause a rally response by others because no physical death has occurred. When someone dies, it is customary, especially in the South, to take food and offer sympathy. People expect grief in that situation and usually react to the loss in helpful ways. The type of grief we experience is often not even recognized by others. However, if the loss IS recognized, people often times do not know what to say or how to respond.

Our grief (A-typical Cyclic Grief) is further complicated because we are also unsure how to express what we feel or experience. Our feelings of guilt, fear of judgment by others, feelings of being disloyal to our children, and shame can cause us to keep our feelings hidden. We tend to grieve in silence.

We love, celebrate, and value our children. It can be emotionally painful to watch them struggle. We often hide this pain because we are unsure how to express our feelings and sometimes feel guilty and confused because of our feelings. Again I want to stress, our children are NOT our source of grief! It is the difficulty of trying to live in a society that places high value on "normal" when you are raising a child that is outside of that "normal". I have heard many parents say, "If I lived on an island, I could live with 'OUR normal' happily ever after.

To borrow an example from Dr. Seuss, the grief is better explained as being caused by trying to raise our little "Sneeches" in a society of "Star-bellied Sneeches" when they have NOT a star on their belly, *The Sneeches and Other Stories* by Dr. Seuss.

This is not to suggest that all people who are living with a child or adult child with a disability will experience every emotion with the same level of intensity or move from one emotion to the next like stepping stones. We all have our own individual journey, however, I do believe we share common emotions, whether brief or long lasting, on this road less traveled.

It would be impossible to fully comprehend what lies ahead, but it is no longer acceptable to not talk about some of the emotional impacts you will or already have encountered on your journey. We are in this together. Learning to adapt to our new normal helps us reduce the amount of time we spend stuck in repeating cycles of unexpected grief.

It is time to break the silence of A-typical Cyclic Grief that naturally occurs for all of us living life outside of "normal." We will watch the cycles unfold through the eyes of a young woman named Lori and her family. We will talk about her experiences and explore our own while being open and raw about our emotions.

The ACG model will help you think about how you have been affected emotionally by the loss of "normal" due to your child's disability. You will learn how to respond to your changing circumstances in healthier ways. The goal is to improve quality of life by adapting to your new journey, rather than trying to get back what has been lost.

If you feel bogged down by all the background information you have been presented with and are wondering why you wasted your money buying this book, just hold on. The worst is over and the best is yet to come. This is as technical as it gets. The rest of the information is easy reading.

In upcoming chapters, we will go in-depth into each emotional stage of grief. Feel free to refer back to the model for an overview of the stages as you read through the rest of the book.

Now let's meet Lori and share her experiences with A-typical Cyclic Grief (ACG). I am confident many of you will find yourselves reflected within the pages ahead. We will work through the stages together. Let's get this elephant out of the center of the room and the center of our lives.

Chapter 1: Small Wonders

It was a raw, cold January day and Lori thought she resembled an engorged tick more than a human. She was in her last month of pregnancy and had gained at least 50 pounds over the course of the past 8 months. She was tired all the time and found it impossible to shave her legs or tie her shoes. She settled on the realization that she would look like Sasquatch in the delivery room but figured no one would really be paying attention to her legs at that point. Her due date was February 6th, which meant she had close to 10 days left, unless she went into labor earlier. Her first child! She was feeling a strong sense of urgency to clean everything and organize the nursery, which is what she had been doing all day.

The pains in her back reminded her that she should probably rest, but she wanted to get a list of things done before Mike got home from work. They were both overjoyed at the idea of becoming parents. She remembered the day they found out she was pregnant. It was not a planned pregnancy, but nonetheless, they could not have been more excited if it were. She and Mike had only been married a month when she became pregnant. They were newlyweds and not fully prepared financially or otherwise to begin a family. But as surprises go, this was the best. Ready or not, they would meet their first born, their son.

They had planned to name him Zechariah, a strong biblical name, since both she and Mike were people of faith. They eventually changed the name to Tommy, deciding that Zechariah might be too problematic during the elementary school years. She prayed daily for her child to be healthy and for God to give them guidance in raising him. She was so exhausted! Time to call it quits, she decided, as she heard Mike's truck pull into the driveway. Mike came through the door looking tired himself. She had stopped working outside the home a few weeks ago, but Mike was still working full time with overtime hours that took him away from home for long periods of time.

They ate dinner and talked about the day. She told Mike all she had accomplished, and he chided her for doing so much in her condition. They both decided to sit down and relax, enjoying an evening together. They were doing pretty well lately. Truth be told, she and Mike did not have the best relationship at times. This first year had been very rocky. Even though they were excited about the baby, they often fought, and Mike was excessively jealous in unhealthy ways. Lori was unsure what to do about it, because more than anything, she wanted their son to have a family that was unbroken. Mike would accuse her of looking at other men, even in her current tick-like state. She had known Mike for years before they married but had not seen this side of him.

She would pray that he would become more secure in their relationship and things would be okay. Her mind drifted back to the day they were attending his work party and Lori felt so uncomfortable, but she could not understand why. It was as if everyone around her knew something she did not. Some secret seemed to be looming and people's faces gave away their strained efforts at concealing whatever it was. Her conversations with others felt awkward which was different from most of her first encounters with people. She was normally very social and could talk to a perfect stranger with ease. It was weird. Maybe it was her insecurity. Still, in the back of her mind, something seemed off. Did Mike talk bad about her to his co workers, she wondered. Surely not! She dismissed the thought as soon as she had it. She simply reminded herself that everyone has insecurities and she needed to be patient with Mike.

The due date came and went and no baby. Not even the beginning signs of labor. In fact, the doctor said she was not even effaced. Not even a little. She had no idea what to expect it was, after all, her first baby. Today marks 9 days past the due date and she is sick. Literally, she is running a fever and feels terrible. Something feels very wrong to her and she is grateful she has a doctor's appointment today. At 4:00 p.m. she is sitting with the doctor who tells her she is still not effaced, but that he wants to run a stress test on the baby. The test reveals the baby is in distress. He apparently was not feeling well either.

The doctor ordered her to go directly to the hospital for admission to induce labor. She called Mike who left work to meet her at the hospital. She also called her mother to join them. Please God, she prayed, let Tommy be okay. Please protect us both. Once she was admitted, she was placed in a room where the first on call OB came in to tell her about this new cutting edge procedure. He went on to explain that he could administer a drug that would cause effacement but a potential side effect could be contractions that would not stop. He talked about the safety of the procedure and how the contractions would be stopped if necessary. He said the baby would not be harmed.

She felt so sick! "Okay", she responded to the doctor, "whatever you think is best." She was then transported to another room to be given an epidural. What a disaster! The anesthetist was completely incompetent and gave her multiple shots, one of which was too high and caused her difficulty breathing. Other professionals were brought in to make sure she was going to be okay. By midnight, she still lay in the hospital bed helpless and feeling weaker by the moment. The new drug did cause contractions that would not stop, so she was given the other drug to stop the effacement procedure. She has not seen a doctor since the contractions were stopped and has no idea what is next.

Mike and her mother are still in the room, both trying to stay awake but fighting sleep in the wee hours of the morning. She looks at the clock which reads 3:00 a.m. She has been on her right side for hours now. Every time she gets in any other position, Tommy goes crazy and the monitor shows his heartbeat stopping. The nurse speculates that he may be on his cord when she switches positions. She asked the last nurse that came in when the doctor will return. She told Lori that the next doctor on call will be in at 7:00 a.m. Fear and fatigue wash over her. Again, she prays.

The next morning, which felt more like a long continuation of the night and day before, finally arrives. Yet another OB comes in, looks at her chart, and announces it is time to induce labor. Lori could not believe her ears. What?! Induce labor?! She was not a doctor, but it seemed pretty logical to her that something more immediate should happen. Her baby was identified as being in distress at 4:00 p.m. yesterday, she can only lie on one side without losing his heartbeat, and effacement was unsuccessful. She is running a fever and feels as if she and her baby are in danger. Neither her mother nor Mike protest against the doctor's suggestion to induce labor, so perhaps they are not sensing the same danger as she?

She is weak, sick, and exhausted but from somewhere deep within Lori speaks up and says no. She respectfully asks the new OB to look at her chart again, including the past 15 hours. The OB did look and ordered an emergency C section. The anesthetist came back in. Again? More medicine? She was pretty sure she had recently been given a dose just under an hour ago. She is wheeled to the delivery room or operating room, she isn't quite sure which. Her body began to shake uncontrollably. What was happening? She did not know. She only knew they were finally bringing Tommy into this world. It all seemed to happen quickly from that point. At last, she would see her son. Please God, she prayed, protect him.

The doctor finally ushered him into this world and Lori thought he was the most beautiful sight she had ever seen. Frightening almost, how much he looked like her. It was like a miniature mirror in one of those fun houses had been placed in front of her when she looked at him. The ones that shrink your head, she thought. She was not able to hold him because the doctors had to complete the C section and he had to be cleaned up. After the procedure, she was sent to recovery, still wildly shaking. No matter how many blankets were placed on her, the shaking did not stop. She did not feel cold. In fact, she did not feel much of anything.

She could overhear the nurses talking. "That poor girl", one said. "That anesthetist should be fired. I bet she gets fired over this one. I heard she is drinking and taking pills." "I can't believe she hasn't already been fired", the other one says. "I hope she is going to be okay. She can't stop shaking. Bless her heart."

Oh no! Lori realizes they are talking about her! Am I okay? She now realizes she felt like something was wrong because something was wrong. Just then a young anesthetist, one she had not seen before, pulls the curtain back and smiles at her. "How are you doing?" he asks. "Okay," she replies with a shaky voice. "I'm going to check a few things then come back *every 15 minutes to check again," he says. "Can you feel this?" he asks as he scrapes the bottom of her foot. "Can you move your legs?" he asks. He checked her breathing and calmly assured her that she would be fine and should stop shaking soon.*

Nearly 36 hours after the C section, she was well enough to care for her baby for the first time. Her fever finally broke, and she was deemed well enough to see him. They had fed him some in the nursery while she was sick. She felt a deep sorrow and guilt that she had missed so many of those precious hours with him. Her mother and Mike seem to know more about him than she does, but that also gives her a sense of comfort to know they have been caring for him while she was unable. She breast fed and could not believe the joy and closeness she felt. She never would have believed it was possible to feel this connected to another human being.

Her mother filmed the nurses cleaning Tommy up after the birth. One of the nurses in the video was asking when his due date was and her mother responded with "February 6th." The nurse whistles and states "that was probably an accurate date. This baby definitely looks close to two weeks past his due date." She is pointing out his deeply wrinkled skin and other aspects that were obvious signs he was in the womb longer than perhaps he should have been. He was born on February 16th, and even though he looked like a wrinkled up little man, he was her little bundle of wrinkles and she loved him beyond measure.

She also felt connected to Mike as she saw the pride in his eyes as he looked at his first- born son. Thank you God, she whispered. Thank you for protecting Tommy. Thank you for protecting me. Mike was looking forward to coaching little league and shared dreams of his son playing sports just like he did. Lori imagined a well-mannered, good-looking, young man that would be kind to others, well liked, and love God above all. Oh, the dreams! It had been a rough start but a beautiful future lay ahead....

Do you remember the day your child was born? What a joyous time. In fact, there really is nothing like it. It is a milestone in our lives that marks the beginning of the next generation. You take on the new role of mom or dad. Something indescribable happens when you see your child for the first time. The overwhelming love that takes your breath away will be the steadfast anchor that helps you get through those middle-of-the-night feedings and perpetual lack of sleep. No matter what, you realize that your life has been changed forever.

I remember feeling like I had finally arrived because I earned the badge of parenthood, as if it was a subset of humanity. A community bound together by diaper bags, lack of sleep, stained clothing, and complete allegiance to their tiny human. I finally understood what it felt like to have a child. It was like the next level of life, at least for me. I felt a sense of commonality with other parents because we shared a similar experience.

Although most of this book will focus on how our differences impact our experiences, it is important to spend some time talking about our similarities. No matter what language you speak, a smile is universal, and it means basically the same thing in every language. The same is true of parenthood. Becoming a parent is a universally understood experience shared by billions across the globe.

As I am writing this book, the elections of 2016 have just ended. The polarization of our great nation is startling. It seems increasingly more difficult for our society to find similarities, common ground, rather than what divides them. We have to learn as parents of children with disability that others cannot see life through our eyes and, therefore, will at times appear insensitive, uncaring, or judgmental.

The majority of people we will encounter mean well but just do not have enough knowledge or insight to understand how to support us. Sometimes their well intended efforts backfire. Here's the point: this book is not meant to divide but rather help us understand our own feelings and reactions, as well as the reactions of our society to move towards commonality. The lack of information about the psychological and emotional impacts does not help bridge the gap. Hopefully, the information found in this book will not only help you as a parent but can also be shared with those "Star-bellied Sneeches" (see introduction) to help them gain insight into our experiences as well.

Our daily interactions in a "normal driven" society can be compared to a hazardous intersection crossing as follows: The intersection where "normal" and NOT collide is dangerous and without working traffic signals. We are unprepared for what may be coming towards us emotionally because we have no signals to follow and the intersection is full of blind-spots. Yet, we cross this intersection sometimes at an hourly rate. Emotional collisions that occur at these daily crossings can feel like the equivalent of a massive wreck with sustainable injuries. Many of these collisions may feel intentional but I believe many are truly accidental due to blind-spots and lack of awareness of our journey. The "normal's" have blind-spots when it comes to our experiences.

I remember talking with a parent one day who was in tears after a conversation with a complete stranger who was helping her load some books she was picking up. This parent has a child with autism and some challenging behaviors. The stranger had no clue about this parent's child and began to rant about these "troubled children" and "kids with learning problems" that are taking away from all those "good kids" and how it's just not fair. He continued to rant to this parent about his grandchild having to put up with a kid in his classroom that appears to be challenged in much the same way as this parent's child.

The parent ended the one-way conversation as quickly as possible to escape the harsh rant that was crushing her soul. She was completely unprepared for that emotional experience. She cried as she talked about the painful impacts of that exchange. His words will be forever burned in her mind, whether she agrees with his opinions or not. Had she not been a parent of a child with autism, perhaps she might have disagreed with his opinion. But his expressed opinion would not have been a source of emotional pain. She crossed paths with someone living the expected "normal" that had no idea she was raising a child that did not fit into the expected norms. The result of that intersection crossing ended in emotional injury. Not every crossing is or will be negative, but for the ones that are, we have to deal with how they affects us.

By working through these emotions, we can explore our own reactions, acknowledge our pain, reframe our experiences, and prepare for future encounters. We can readjust our own perspectives and define our own norms. This can lead to better adapting, stronger families, and ultimately a healthier quality of life. Whether your child has just recently been diagnosed or you have been on this path for years, you are NOT alone.

In 2016, the CDC states, "One in six children in the United States have one or more developmental disabilities or other developmental delays." The U.S. News & World Report 2016, states "United States census estimates indicate the population is at 322,762,018 in 2016."

If one in six children in the United States have one or more developmental disability or delay, it would insinuate that a large number of parents are experiencing an A-typical journey of parenthood. The A-typical Cyclic Grief journey is real. We do NOT have to struggle in silence! There is hope and emotional healing for a brighter future.

Chapter 2: "Normal" or Not?

Lori is busy in the kitchen making lunch for Tommy. Her heart is full as she glances over to see him watching his favorite cartoon with the most beautiful smile on his face. Tommy has grown into a very handsome 2 ½ year old with blonde hair and dazzling green eyes. His olive complexion gives him a flawless appearance, almost doll-like. He is often mistaken for a girl, so she is careful to dress him in rugged clothes because she refuses to cut his beautiful blonde curls just yet.

She was just about to call him into the kitchen, when she heard him talking in the other room. It sounded like he was repeating a phrase or name, she wasn't sure. She playfully ran into the other room, excited to hear him talk. "What Tommy? What did you say?" No response. He just kept watching the cartoon as if she wasn't in the room. That seemed to happen often. When he was younger, she realized he would not answer when she called his name, even though she had coached him to reply. She was so concerned that she had spoken with Mike about it several times. He finally agreed to get Tommy's hearing checked, so they did. But the doctor told them everything was fine. His hearing was perfectly fine.

She picked Tommy up, hugged him, and carried him into the kitchen to eat lunch. She was trying something new again today, but had the backup ready just in case. He sat at the bar bouncing as if he were on an invisible trampoline. "Look sweetie," Lori said, "I made you something really good. Just take one bite, please, for mommy." He immediately started to gag just at the site of the macaroni and cheese in front of him. Lori knew it was a lost cause.

Her mind drifted back to that day in the pediatrician's office when she told him that Tommy would not eat anything other than baby food without any lumps. He was a year and a half old and should have been eating table food by then or at least solids. He would gag and literally throw up every time she tried to introduce something new. The doctor assured her she was giving up too soon. "Just put the food in front of him and he will eat it when he gets hungry enough. Give him lots of choices." So she did for nearly two days. For nearly two days,

Tommy did not eat and was beginning to look ill with dark circles under his eyes.

She just knew instinctively there was more to this than a picky eater. Despite the doctor's recommendations, she fed her baby the only thing he would eat, baby food. As she glanced back up at her now 2 ½ year old, she sighed and tossed the macaroni into the trash as she pulled out brown sugar and cinnamon pop tarts. At least at 2 ½, he eats more than just baby food, she thought. He grabbed the pop tarts and began to eat as if he was starving. As of late, this was the mainstay of his diet. A wave of guilt and worry washed over her as she heard him repeating phrases that did not make sense and were not aimed at her or anyone for that matter.

She now recognizes the phrases as lines from the movies he insists on watching over and over again. She also notices that when he comes home from preschool, he mimics the teacher. She can always tell which child got in trouble the most because Tommy is like a recorder and someone somewhere is pushing play. She hears him frequently stating, "no-no Katie no-no," using the teacher's same tone and pitch. It is actually quite eerie. If only that preschool teacher knew she was being recorded by her tiny student. Lori marvels at her son's memory. Yet, she is increasingly more concerned about his odd behavior.

She asked the pediatrician about his language development and was assured that sometimes boys develop later than girls. He told her not to worry and give it more time. Tommy had met all his developmental milestones or so Lori thought. She can still remember his first steps like it was yesterday. Other than his odd usage of language and strange forms of play, he was the typical toddler. But still the nagging worry never left her mind. She used to share her concerns with Mike. At first, he gave her assurance and told her she worried too much. Lately, he is becoming increasingly more annoyed, accusing her of looking for something that isn't there.

Actually, he is annoyed most days, at least with her, for almost everything. The accusations have only become worse over time. He is obsessed with thoughts that Lori is cheating on him or that she is always looking at other men. He calls her names and puts her down frequently. If she wears lipstick, he accuses her of trying to look good for someone else. Sometimes it feels like a losing battle. He accuses her of being obsessed with Tommy and tells her he is tired of talking about Tommy all the time. Sometimes he will apologize. He says he does not know why he acts the way he does. But the cycle continues.

Mike worked a lot, so he wasn't with Tommy nearly as much as Lori. On good days, he and Tommy would wrestle when he came home from work, like most sons and fathers. To Mike, he appeared to be the typical toddler in many aspects and the odd or unusual behaviors were easily dismissed because he was "only 2 and ½ years old." Lori began to keep her fears to herself mainly to avoid conflicts with Mike and maybe, if she's being honest, to avoid the thoughts that something could be wrong. After all, it is comforting to believe that everything is fine and that she might just be over-reacting. She prayed for God to heal Tommy if something was wrong and tried to have faith that everything was okay.

Bedtime routines were grueling, and many nights were spent lying with Tommy for hours waiting for him to fall asleep. He stopped taking naps at 6 months old. He would stay up for 12 to 13 hours and still be wide awake. His only comfort at night was watching Pure Country, a popular movie about a country singer trying to find himself. He seemed to love the music but would lie still for long periods of time watching the credits roll across the screen over and over and over again. He would cry if the credits stopped and push Lori's hand towards the remote to rewind. Many nights this was Tommy's highway to dreamland. Lori wanted to scream or pull her hair out at the thought of watching that movie AGAIN. She vowed to burn it once he grew out of this obsession or weird form of a sleep aid. It was a good movie but enough was enough!

Usually, by the time Tommy was asleep, both Lori and Mike had passed out as well. Without babysitters available to them, the only time they had together was after he went to sleep. Nowadays, that time was never. It was beginning to make a rocky marriage worse. Lori did not know how to fix it and was beginning to feel resentful towards Mike for his unwillingness to listen to her concerns and his constant unwarranted accusations. After all, she was the one who spent all day with Tommy. If anyone should know if something seemed off, it would be her. How would she ever have time to be unfaithful? What did she ever do to deserve this mistrust and suspicion? It seemed as if Mike believed that eventually she would leave him or be unfaithful. It's as if he had predetermined that she would abandon him and was acting as if it had already happened.

Mike would complain about Tommy's sleep patterns and began to make up excuses about why he could not spend time with Tommy alone. He would say that he did not understand what Tommy needed because he could not tell him. It was true. Tommy did not have the use of language that most toddlers have. Therefore, in order to understand him, you had to know his patterns and rituals well. Lori had no idea how to make Tommy take naps, go to sleep, or teach him to talk beyond all the things she had already tried. He had such narrow interests and wanted to do the same things over and over again. Sometimes she wasn't even sure how to discipline him. Did he even understand?

She reflects back on the day she had decided Tommy needed more time with other toddlers beyond just preschool. She was still relatively new to their town but she had met a friendly girl and fellow stay-at-home mom who offered to get together some time. She decided to take her up on the offer and planned a play date. Her mind replayed the first time she met Susan. She was so friendly and warm. She had a daughter who was a year older than Tommy. A chill ran down her spine, as she thinks about the dreadful play date.

It is now several months later, and Lori finds herself reeling from that experience. She remembers it as if it was yesterday. The day started out pretty good. They took the kids to the park, and they seemed to be enjoying the slides and other playground adventures together. They all went back to Lori's house after the park, and it all went downhill from there. Tommy was thirsty, hungry, and tired. He pulled Lori's hand to whatever it was he needed. He didn't ask for anything. He could use a lot of words, but it was more like he was in some sort of play, reciting his lines over and over. When it came to everyday, *purposeful language, it wasn't there or he couldn't access it.*

*Susan's three year old daughter was pushy and
demanding as many toddlers tend to be. She had several
tantrums and Susan would give in to her bad behavior just to
calm her down. Her daughter was very verbal, unlike Tommy.
In fact, she would frequently tell her mother "no" and other
things that made Lori grateful for Tommy's quiet nature. Tommy
was demanding in his own way, though. He would jerk Lori in
many different directions to fling her hand towards something he
wanted or needed help with. It was his version of verbal
demands. Lori assumed Susan understood as she was fighting
her own similar battles. She felt connected, less isolated in a way,
to watch another mother struggle with behaviors that were
challenging.*

*After several hours of being home, Susan spoke up and
said, "I can't stand this! I like you and I am glad that we are
becoming friends but I can't stand to be around your child! He is
like a little monster that is out of control!" What??? Lori was
shocked! She was emotionally devastated by the hurtful words
just slung her direction. She couldn't imagine someone would
see her child or any child that way. "What do you mean?," Lori
asked. Susan went on, "He just pulls you around like you're
some kind of puppet and you let him." Susan sounded angry.
Lori felt attacked. She tried so hard to teach him to talk, but she
knew the only way he could communicate his needs was by
showing her. She felt so embarrassed and stunned by her new
friend's remarks. She literally felt physical pain, as if someone
had just punched her in the gut.*

*She fought the urge to cuss Susan out on the spot or
worse. She was overcome with the need to defend her baby.
How dare this woman come into my house and call my child a
monster, she thought. She quickly made some excuse about why
the play date would have to be cut short and they soon parted
ways. Once she left, Lori decided their friendship would not
work out because she wasn't sure she wanted to be friends with
someone who could be so cruel. Again, she felt anger towards
Susan for her insulting remarks. If you don't want to be around
Tommy, then I don't want to be around you, were her exact*

thoughts. She and Tommy would just spend their days together. After all, he has cousins that play with him, and even though they are older, they are still companionship. What a nightmare that social experiment turned out to be, she thought to herself!

She catches an object out of the corner of her eye, as her mind snaps back to the present, realizing Tommy is doing his "fly bys." She wishes so desperately that she could get inside his head to understand him better. He carefully moves the pop tart box to the corner of the bar. Then he moves his eye repetitively past the corner, looking at the box with his peripheral vision. Back and forth he passes, as if in a deep trance. He does this frequently with any object he can place at the corner of the bar. What does he see? What is he thinking? He lines up his index finger with his thumb forming a 90 degree angle and places it in front of the box as if to measure the box. He appears to be a miniature architect or quality control inspector. He is two years old! Is he a genius, she wonders? "What are you doing, Tommy?" "What do you see?" she asked. No response. She kisses his forehead and whispers, "I love you."

Is he okay? What if something is wrong? The thoughts flood her mind. Her worries are overwhelming at times. When the doubt and fear rises to the surface, it feels like someone is kicking her in the gut. It hurts so deeply she can barely stand the pain. Why? Why do I feel such intense pain? Do I already know the answer to those questions, but I just don't want to face them? NO! She chides herself. Mike is right. I am over reacting and worry too much. Tommy is okay... Please God she prayed!

She scoops Tommy up and the deep love she feels the moment she holds Tommy close in her arms overrides her doubt, frustrations, and even fears. "I love you Tommy." "I am so proud of my little boy," she whispers. "We will always have each other," she says as she pulls him in closer. Her love has only grown more intense with time. She imagined all mothers feel this type of love and worry about their children from time to time. Still she knew deep down inside that her worries went beyond the typical toddler worries. But nonetheless she assures herself that what she feels is normal and Tommy will catch up...

We can see the emotional struggles bubbling to the surface in Lori's life, although it is not yet clear if Tommy has a disability. It is clear that she is grateful for Tommy and loves him very much, regardless. Perhaps Tommy is simply delayed. We will find out as the story unfolds in future chapters. However, it is also clear that even the suspicion that something could be "wrong" is causing an emotional reaction in both Lori and Mike.

Lori has encountered people that have said harsh things, causing her emotional pain. She is dealing with those incidents while at the same time trying to cope with the emotional pain of her own fears.

I, like Lori, was never ungrateful for my son, but the sadness and emotional turmoil at times was overwhelming. Still, I found myself pushing on and grieving in silence. These encounters build year after year and cause an emotional cycle of reactions that can negatively impact many areas of our lives. My emotional upheaval began as early as my son's pre-school years, prior to his diagnosis.

One of my most vivid memories of my son's preschool years was his fourth birthday party. It was the dead of winter and very cold outside so no outdoors party and I definitely did not want 15 four year olds inside with cake. So, I planned a party at the local skating rink. You could rent a side room; bring in cake, plus pay a fee for your party to trash the rink and clean up was included. It was a win! I had been forewarned about the risk of planning birthday parties by other moms. Of course, the greatest risk being that no one would show up. It was a chance I was willing to take. I thought my cute little blond four year old deserved a party. After all, he would only turn four once right?

The morning of the party, I arrived early to set up the party room and make sure all the arrangements were finalized. The invitations had been given to every child in my son's preschool class. We were inclusive of all. He did not seem to have any friendship preferences. His speech was still very limited and he exhibited odd behaviors. During my frequent visits to the preschool, I had learned he was both the teacher's and class pet.

15

Every day he would come into the classroom and seek out a little wooden puzzle piece of a horse. I don't know what it was but he was obsessed with horses back then! He would carry the horse with him all day while at preschool until it was time to leave to go home. He commonly sat in the teachers lap during story time and usually could be found on the playground doing his own thing. He was typically alone on the outer edges, while the other kids played together. They were not purposely leaving him out; rather he found other things more interesting than his classmates. I was never entirely sure how much he really interacted with the other kids, so the birthday party attendance was up in the air. I prayed!

By 10:30 a.m., several of his classmates and their parents had arrived. YES! I was elated. At least a few came. My son Jacob didn't seem to notice, but each child, in turn, ran over to him and hugged him. My heart was melting. By 11:00 a.m., all but one child had arrived. I could not believe it really. No one expects that high of attendance, but I was not complaining. The kids all played and skated together laughing. It seemed as if they took turns coming by to talk to Jacob and encouraging him to come skate with them. It was almost time to open presents, and the last child arrived late. I will never forget it!

Ben was a good size four year old bounding in with his grandfather in tow. His grandfather approached me and apologized for being late. He explained they were at a family function and had not intended to come to the party, but Ben had gotten so upset, so he agreed to bring him. He went on to say they had to stop to buy a birthday gift and that is what had taken so long. He told me he just did not understand, but Ben insisted that they had to find a toy horse to buy for Jacob. He said they had to stop three places but finally found a horse. Tears started to well in my eyes. I knew why he insisted on a horse. His grandfather remarked as he was walking off, "Your boy must really like horses."

I had invited his preschool teacher, who came as well, and I was so thankful. She had a way with those four year olds that I did not. It was cake and present time, so we all gathered into the party room to sing happy birthday and open presents. It was

16

adorable. But I was not prepared for what came next. Jacob still needed help opening presents and would easily lose focus. Needless to say, he had plenty of volunteers to help. One by one, each present was opened, and one by one, a horse marched out of the package. It was like a herd. All different types; plastic, stuffed, puzzles, and figurines were unwrapped. Admittedly, I think one of them might have been a leopard, but it was the thought that counted.

Everyone in that party room was moved and slightly confused, especially the parents of the other four year olds. But the teacher and I shared a knowing glance and were both touched. Not only did every single one of his classmates attend, they all bought him the one thing they knew he loved, because they had watched him each day as he held tightly to his horse. It took everything I had to contain the waterworks that were threatening to flow right then and there! I could hardly believe it. It was the sweetest display of kindness, thoughtfulness, and acceptance I had witnessed in a long time.

I was overwhelmed with joy and deeply sad at the same time. My sweet blond boy was oblivious to all of it. He appeared uninterested to connect with this group of kids all reaching out to him. But I knew it wasn't a lack of interest. It was lack of ability. He was locked away somewhere deep within himself, only peeking out at times. Somehow these very young children seemed to know that and loved him anyway, just the way he was. Deep in my soul, I felt sorrow and fear, but I also felt joy and hope. *Sometimes the grief emotions are mixed with feelings of intense love and joy all at the same time.*

My son had not yet been formally diagnosed with autism, but it had become obvious something was wrong. He was not developing normally. I was reacting to a loss that had not been formally labeled yet. It was penetrating every aspect of my life. The fear of the unknown was like a looming dark figure that I couldn't quite make out, chilling me to the bone.

As I stated earlier, a developmental disability marks the loss of "normal" that we all expect when we have children. Our expectations, hopes, and dreams all come into question. It causes a grief response.

Sometimes we may feel guilty for feeling sad. It is a very weird feeling to grieve over the living. It can cause a state of emotional conflict. When a physical death has occurred, people do not feel guilty for grieving over the loss of their loved one, and it is socially acceptable for them to grieve. Grief over your child that is alive, and most likely physically healthy, is not the type of grief people are equipped to respond to in supportive ways.

This can lead to feeling disconnected from those around you. I remember feeling very isolated at my son's birthday party, even though I was surrounded by kind, loving people. Even family and close friends may not fully relate to your grief because they have children that are typical and fall within the expected norms. They may feel compassion but not be fully able to understand all of the painful emotions you are experiencing at times. As stated above, grief emotions can be mixed with feelings of intense love and joy all at the same time.

During my research in graduate school, I found the term "chronic sorrow" in an article written by Olshansky (1962), a counselor to parents of children with a disability. He introduced the term "chronic sorrow" in the early 1960s when he described the normal psychological response in the suffering of parents dealing with mentally disabled children.

Teel, another professional, also wrote on the subject in 1991, where she talks about understanding the impacts of "chronic grief" when helping patients caring for developmentally disabled children. Interestingly enough, the information was written to assist professionals helping parents that were raising a child with a developmental disability. It was not written directly to the parents who were raising children with disabilities. Teel was writing from the nursing field and Olshansky from the counseling field.

As you can see a few pioneers recognized and wrote about a cyclic grief process years ago in professional journals to share with other professionals. I have incorporated some of their foundational insights, which have helped shape the development of the A-typical Cyclic Grief Model. I am grateful for their contributions and recognition of some of the unique aspects of the grief we experience. We need to know that it is okay and common to grieve as well. It really is okay and should be expected. It does not mean you do not love your child! We grieve for our children and with our children, even if they are unable to grieve for themselves.

Whether you have been on this path for years or just recently learned of your child's disability, it is common for you to feel sad and uncertain about the future. But you will also find you have many years of joy and laughter ahead as well. Embrace your feelings but hold on to the hope that whatever the future holds it can be good. Different doesn't equal bad. I hope you are finding some validation and relief to know that you are not alone as we move forward in our exploration of A-typical Cyclic Grief (ACG).

Chapter 3: The Yesteryears: A Field of Dreams.

It was a beautiful morning. The sun was bright against the clear blue morning sky. It was the perfect opportunity to have a cup of coffee on the patio, while Tommy was sleeping. Lori kicked back in the chaise lounge chair, enjoying the sounds of nature. The birds were singing, the air was cool, and the large oak was providing just the right amount of shade. She stares off into the deep blue sky, as she thinks about her youth, when times were simpler. The worries that seemed so big back then, seem so trivial now. Her mind drifts back to middle school.

She woke up in a panic. The first day of eighth grade! She had heard all the rumors of what they do to eighth graders on the first day. She even heard they made some kids swallow oysters with a string attached, and then pull them back up. The thought made her sick.

It had been a pretty good summer. They spent time in Tennessee where her father was still working. They came home just in time for back to school activities.

It was a bright, sunny day in the south, as usual for that time of year. She looked out of her bedroom window to see the palm trees and sunshine welcoming her to this new day.

She was only 12 years old and most of the kids were a good year older than she, allowing both her age and size to be used against her. She had an olive complexion, green eyes, and dirty blonde hair. She was described as cute frequently because she was so tiny. She barely weighed ninety-five pounds soaking wet. At five feet and one inch tall, teachers called her pet names like "little bit" and "tadpole," which only emphasized her smallness. She was petite and hoped she would fill out a little more. The sooner the better!

She climbed out of bed, forcing down breakfast, then hustling to get ready for her first day of school. The new school! She got dressed only to realize the one pair of new pants her mother bought her over the summer break shrank and were now too short!!! Oh no!! This is terrible. She began to cry. She already felt insecure because she never had the cute, fashionable clothes, like the other girls, making her stand out.

Her mother told her she was acting ridiculous and no one

would notice her pants being too short. She was sure her mother was wrong, but she had no other choices. She had made it through her past years of school wearing clothes that were not "cool." Her mother would clothe her in hand sewn dresses and matching shorts outfits bought at inexpensive stores. She knew that eighth grade meant a higher standard and the kids would be less friendly to kids that didn't dress "cool." Everyone knew the first day was the most important. Here we go again, she thought.

Off she went. It was a brisk walk to the bus stop, maybe a half mile. She had to cross an eight-lane major highway. Thank goodness there was a button and crosswalk. She lived right off a thoroughfare for big trucks. She had a lot of respect for that highway.

She remembered the time when she was ten years old and she was riding her bike to her friend's house. She was on the sidewalk that lined the highway. It was narrow in many spots and cracked with mounds that popped up out of the concrete creating mini ramps. Her bike hit one of those ramps, sending her out onto the highway, directly into the path of an oncoming truck. She was able to get back on the sidewalk just in the nick of time. Her heart had never beaten so fiercely. The memory still gives her chills.

The light changed calling her back into the present. She crossed the highway and made it to the bus stop in about 10 minutes. She caught the bus and rode to school with several other students who were picked up at the same bus stop.

Several hours later, she was on her way home, relieved that she had not had to swallow anything. Really, it all seemed to be a bunch of hype to scare newbies like her, she thought. She had been right about the pants though. All day long she wanted to become invisible, because she felt that every glance in her direction was spotlighting her too small pants. She heard several students whispering and laughing at her during class changes. She even heard the word "high-waters" and no one wanted to be caught dead in high-waters.

As she was walking home, she heard one of the girls, a big girl from her bus stop, start making fun of her pants. She wanted to cry on the spot, but she was far too prideful for that.

21

She twirled around and told that girl to shut-up! The big girl was about to kill her until another girl stepped in and took up for her. She liked this girl right away.

Denise invited her over. They lived just down the street from one another. She offered her clothes to borrow for school. Believe it or not, they were close to the same size. They became fast friends and her social life took a turn in a new direction. Denise was a popular, pretty girl with lots of friends. Her mother never seemed to notice that she was wearing Denise's clothes to school every day. Thank God for her friend. She knew deep down that her life would have been very different in school if it had not been for her. School was not a kind place for poor kids, kids of lesser intelligence, and kids with special needs, or those that seemed weird or different.

Several years later, as an older teen, she got a part-time job and bought her own wardrobe. She had a great bunch of friends that still all hung out together in the neighborhood, even though they went to separate high schools.

One day, while she was out running errands, she passed a middle school girl wearing high-waters. She only noticed because she had to stoop down to pick up something she had dropped. She noticed the girl avoided looking her in the eye and looked as if she wanted to disappear. She felt a twinge of pain seeing herself reflected in that little girl as she remembered her own experience a few years ago.

She thought about the kids at school that are on the fringes. She feels sad for them. She thinks about how her social experience might have been so different if she would have had to wear clothes that made her stand out or not fit it. She had been teased in elementary school and knew what it felt like to be picked on. She did not ever want to be viewed in that way again. If she was being honest, it left her feeling very insecure on the inside, no matter how she appeared on the outside now.

Now as a senior, she is wearing a beautiful class ring and practicing for graduation. She turned seventeen this year and still weighs less than one hundred pounds. On her tippy-toes she is a solid 5'2. She has grown into the idea that she is petite and admits it has its advantages at times. It has been a great year.

Lots of memories and good times with friends, a year she will never forget. She was voted most likely to succeed and most likely to own her own business. She laughs at that one. Her boyfriend, Daniel, a star football player, plans to go away for college. She wanted to go with him, but will only go locally, as her parents would not let her go away for school. She is sad that they are going to different colleges, but they have agreed to see each other as often as possible.

She is still friends with Denise and the gang and imagines she will always be bonded to them in a special way. She is graduating with honors and her parents are proud. She almost can't believe it is all coming to an end. She is off to college and beyond. She feels like an adult, and it is both scary and exciting. She is terrified at the prospect of a new school environment and having to find her place again. But she is ready to move on with her life and become her own person. She still shrinks inside when she thinks about another first day. She wonders if she will ever feel secure deep down.

Her older brother did not finish high school, and instead chose to get his GED. In 1983, that was still somewhat acceptable, especially if it was to speed up the process of going to work at the family business. He was a popular boy with lots of friends. Their parents owned several businesses that her brother had interest in but Lori did not. Neither one of their parents had gone to college but managed to do quite well. Her brother decided to follow in their footsteps. Their parents had never been divorced, and she did not see that in their future. They would argue occasionally, but outside of that, they seemed to be pretty happy with one another. Lori thought it looked like a good life for her brother and one he wanted for himself. She had other plans.

She and her brother were only one grade apart in school, so their friends overlapped frequently. Several of his friends had also opted for a GED and full time employment instead of the college route. One of his friends named Mike had admitted to having a crush on Lori for years, but nothing ever blossomed until much much later. Mike graduated from a public school instead of taking the GED pathway. She graduated from a private school, so she was only around him at her house or local teen gatherings. However, this proved ample enough time to develop a good friendship. Mike was good-looking, popular, and a fantastic soccer player. He was a couple years older than Lori but only a grade above her in school.

She and Mike were good friends and remained friends through the years. After he graduated from high school, he pursued a trade that led him to a decent paying job and future career. Mike grew up with four siblings and his family was pretty close. His mother was very sweet and kind. Lori had met her on several occasions. She had divorced his father when he was young and remarried Mike's stepfather some years later. They were an average American blended family. He did not remember much about his biological father but knew it had not been a healthy relationship for his mother; he had shared with Lori at one time.

He had confided in Lori as their friendship grew, telling her that when he married one day, he would not ever get a divorce. He told her he would never leave his children like his father had done. Mike had no contact with his biological father and had not since he was very young, prior to the divorce. He felt abandoned by his father and it had shaped his view of parenthood in negative ways. It had left him feeling insecure and not good enough. He said he never understood what he did wrong to make his dad not want anything to do with him. He swore to be different but didn't know exactly what it felt like to be bonded with a father.

He also talked at times about how his father was always accusing his mother of cheating on him, even though, according to Mike, she would never have done so. He said he could remember his father yelling at his mother and his older brother intervening. It sounded like an abusive relationship to Lori, but she wouldn't dare say that to Mike. She only listened. He talked about his mother like she was a saint.

His mother tried to make up for the loss. She was at every sporting event and was known as a short order cook for whatever each child wanted. She loved them dearly and did her best to give them everything they wanted or needed. She was not a

*strong disciplinarian. She was an accommodator. Mike's view
of a mother and wife was forming as he watched his mother cook
for his stepfather and cater to the rest of the family. His
stepfather was demanding and negative, frequently complaining
instead of appreciating. By Lori's assessment, Mike's mother
seemed like a master at covering up and smoothing everything
over.*

*The years passed, and Lori found herself working for a
local company after she decided to take a break from college for
a while. She had developed several new work friendships that
kept her busy socially. She was active and very independent;
partly due to the fact that she had spent many years at home
alone while her parents were building their businesses.*

*Even in her early teens, it was not uncommon for her to
be home alone until late in the night, finding her own meals for
dinner. She spent much of her time talking to friends on the
phone when she was alone. Now as an adult, she still finds
herself talking on the phone a lot at night and feels slightly
uncomfortable with being alone. She and Daniel had broken up
several years before after each realized that long distance
relationships were not so great and both had grown apart. They
parted as friends but really never kept in touch.*

*One night she was out with friends and ran into Mike.
She had not seen him for some time, so they exchanged numbers
and set a time to catch up. They met for coffee and talked for
hours about old times and their current lives. Mike asked Lori
out on an official date that night and she accepted. This is where
the much later part comes in. The date marked the beginnings of
a relationship that eventually led to marriage. Mike and Lori
merge their separate lives into one. This merger brings together
all their life experiences which shape their views and
expectations of the future. These hopes and dreams will become
the standard they build their foundation on. It is their roadmap
or schemas of what is to come. It is their field of dreams.*

Merriam-Webster defines schemas (plural) as the
organization of experiences in the mind or brain that includes a
particular organized way of perceiving cognitively and

responding to a complex situation or set of stimuli. In plain English, it basically means that schemas are formed by the information we take in through our life experiences. An example may be that you developed a schema that all homeless people are lazy because you knew a few homeless people that were unwilling to work. Because of your schema, you will respond to homeless people in ways that support your belief about them. You will look for information that supports your belief and may even reject any information that disagrees with your perspective.

We all develop schemas about family roles, family functioning, siblings, social and economic classes, and so on. Think about Mike. His outline or schema about how a mother is supposed to act towards her husband and children has been largely shaped by his own experiences with his mother. If he meets a mother who forces her children to eat whatever she has cooked for dinner instead of being a short order cook, he may see this as cold and uncaring. He defined his mother's behavior as the "way" a mother should be. He also might view an overbearing or overprotective father as good because his schema of a bad father is an absent one.

Our schemas are shaped by all of our life experiences, including our social experiences from our school years. Since this book is not meant to be an academic exploration of schema formation, we are not going to go in-depth or worry about all the intricate details of the psychological explanation. The important thing to understand is that our minds will store information that we take in through our experiences and create definitions we will later use when we encounter those same or similar situations. Our knowledge and experiences shapes our expectations and our behavior.

One of the things I explore first when I am working with a couple is their family of origin experiences. In other words, I have them describe their parents' relationship towards each other and towards them. Who did what in the home? How did they discipline? When people marry, they are bringing their own definitions of marriage with them. Those definitions, or schemas as we call them, are shaped through their own unique experiences and exposures growing up. When couples have been raised in opposite home lives, it can create problems in the marriage because their expectations or definitions of who does what are very different. How they discipline, spend their time, money, marital roles, household responsibilities, and spirituality are all potential hotspots for unmet expectations.

Unmet expectations generate strong negative emotions that can lead to an overwhelming feeling of dissatisfaction. I remember once talking with a couple who had argued about the same issue for years and admittedly were full of resentment. The wife believed he had not given his all and he felt unfairly accused when such statements were made. In fact, he felt unappreciated for all his efforts. She felt unsupported, invalidated, and misunderstood. Eventually, we were able to pinpoint the problem. I asked her to define "all in" and she gave a wonderful description of being completely submersed with only one focus. To her, this meant nothing else was important except that one focus. She wanted to talk about the one focus constantly, giving all financial resources and attention to reach the goal of said focus.

Her husband was visibly shaken by her definition. He said, "Well according to that definition, she is right. I wasn't all in." The look on her face showed the evidence that she had finally been validated, hearing the words she had longed for. The accusations made sense to him for the first time. He shared that his definition of "all in" meant he was willing but it would not consume them. So, he would avoid conversations about the topic and find ways to distract her from the topic just to find some balance. She read this as him not being all in.

It's clear that our internal definitions or schema that we form and attach to words, phrases, roles, and experiences largely affects how we behave in response. It also largely shapes what we expect from others. Think about when you were in early elementary school. Yes, I realize this may be a stretch for some of us, but give it a go.

Remember when you first started realizing there was a social hierarchy? Teasing and bullying show up on the scene. Most of us probably learned pretty quickly that being different could create some problems socially. We may have tried hard to stay out of the spotlight or tried to fit in to avoid negative teasing or bullying. We started to define "different" as negative through those experiences.

It's not necessarily because we thought "different" was bad, but rather, what happened to kids who were "different" was bad. As an adult looking back, we can view things through a more mature lens and understand that children can be unkind and act out for a variety of reasons. Nonetheless, we still have the negative attachment to being "different" in the school setting based on our own experiences.

In general terms, we define "normal" by what is expected and accepted in our culture or society. When we have children, we have a "normal" schema which we believe our children should follow from birth through adulthood. "Normal" is the usual, the average. Most all of our friends moved out of home at a certain age and went on to lead their own lives separately from their parents. As teenagers, it is what is expected. We all anticipate the norm!

Of course, the loss of "normal" will cause fears and worries for our children on lots of fronts. Think about the differences in childhood we learned to fear. We feared all differences that brought on teasing or any form of negative attention that was hurtful. The fear of not being accepted by others and the behaviors that will be aimed at those who are outcast are burned into our schemas. If you did not experience it firsthand, then you surely witnessed it done to others.

We not only lose "normal" and the familiar schema we know, but we also are faced with the fears of being "different", not only for our children but as parents. Will they be liked by other kids? Will they be teased? Will I be stared at or judged by other parents? Will they be able to….? You can fill in the many blanks. This is important for us to understand because it impacts our emotional reactions to the loss of "normal" at every juncture. Our individual schemas will cause us to be less tolerant of things and more tolerant of other things depending on our own experiences.

Think about both Lori and Mike. Lori will likely feel very strongly about her child being dressed well and accepted by the other children. Fitting in! Mike will likely feel very strongly about his child playing sports and fitting into a team of his peers. Neither Mike nor Lori will want their child to be teased, bullied, and or rejected by other kids. No parent does! But different means nonconformity. To fit in, you have to conform to the norms of your culture. To stand out is okay, but many of us are conditioned through our life experiences to fit in.

When you have a child with a developmental disability, there are many feats in this life you will attain. One of those feats is learning how to thrive and help them thrive in a society where they will not fit in. We do not fit in. Our journey is different! Their journey is different! Different is not less than! It really is okay not to fit in. It really is okay to live life outside the "normal" limits. Take some time to answer the following challenge questions to help you think about your own definitions and experiences and how they may impact your parenting and personal journey of raising a child with differences.

Challenge Questions:

1. **What were your elementary school years like? Were you bullied, teased, left out? Were you a bully at times? How did you see other kids treat kids with disabilities or differences?**

2. **Are you overly sensitive because of negative past experiences? Does it cause you to overreact in certain situations?**

3. **What was your family of origin like? How did they respond to individuals with disabilities?**

4. **How do you envision your role as a mother or father? What is your parenting schema?**

5. **What insecurities or fears do you still carry that have been shaped by your early experiences?**

6. How do you feel like your schema is affecting your parenting? If kids who are raised properly are supposed to act in a certain way and your child is not conforming due to a disability rather than poor parenting, do you still fault yourself as a bad parent? Do you avoid public or social situations that would highlight the differences?

7. How does it influence your behaviors, confidence levels, and beliefs in society?

8. How does your schema differ from your spouse or partner's? What is their schema or expectation in raising children?

9. Talk to your spouse or partner to explore your definitions and expectations both of each other and your children.

10. What does your "different" look like and how is it different from what you expected?

11. How can you learn to embrace the difference and gain an appreciation of it? There are really cool aspects of our kids that are only present because of their exceptionality.

Remember: Our journey is different. Our child's journey is different. Different is not less than! It really is okay not to fit in. It really is okay to live life outside the "normal" limits.

Chapter 4: What Kind of A Parent Am I?

The screaming began on cue. She looked back to see Tommy in his car seat as he realized they were headed to the pediatrician's office. He hated to go! He had memorized the landscape, and just like a faithful alarm clock going off the second the drugstore sign came into view, the alarm rang. She never knew which doctor she would get, so it was like a potluck. She got Tommy out of the car seat and began looking at the sea of cars around her, reminding herself that it would be a long torturous wait. She wanted to wail along with Tommy, but she was pretty sure it would call attention she did not want. These days, she did all she could to avoid public attention. It seemed that Tommy brought enough for the both of them.

She signed him in with one hand as she held him on her hip with the other. It was a balancing act, and he was not light. She knew better than to put him down. She found a seat off in the corner that was open. The waiting room was busy and sick, whiny kids were plentiful. She was grateful that Tommy did not whine. In fact, often it was hard to tell if he was sick or in pain, because he simply did not complain. Maybe, she thought, because he did not have the words to complain, but this thought caused her a deep pain in her gut.

She always hated being stuck in public for any length of time due to Tommy's behavior. Tommy would start staring at things in odd ways or say things over and over loudly at times. She could feel the stares of people. It made her so uncomfortable. It was embarrassing. The feelings were similar to what she felt in middle school when kids were staring at her because she was dressed weird. Sometimes, she wanted to disappear and take Tommy with her. She felt so ashamed of her feelings. It just seemed wrong to feel embarrassed by your child's behavior, especially when he couldn't help it. She hated the awkward stares, and worse, the failed attempts to conceal their stares when she glanced in their direction.

After two hours in the waiting room, finally they were called back and put in a room. Lori sucked in a deep breath. They were going to be seen by the oldest and grouchiest doctor on staff. Truth be told, he probably should have retired 100

31

years ago. He was gruff, with no bedside manner. He seemed to have no patience with Tommy. A trip to the doctor's office for Tommy meant being held down, because he was not able to understand or follow directions. So, if they needed to check his throat or ears, he has to be restrained. Last time they saw this particular doctor, he scratched Tommy's throat and retorted that he needed to learn to be still.

Tommy was already on edge thanks to a two hour wait racked with anxiety. She wasn't doing much better. The door opened and in walked the doctor, complete with scowl on his face. Tommy reached up for Lori to pick him up, desperate for reassurance. She picked him up, trying to help him feel more at ease. At three and a half years old, he was not a lightweight anymore.

She was close to leaving. If it had not been for the fact that Tommy was really sick and needed care, she would have bolted. As the doctor approached, Tommy panicked. Lori was holding on to him with all her might. He moved close enough to look at Tommy's ear, and in one swift move, Tommy hunched his backside up, using Lori as leverage, and landed a perfect side kick right in the Grinch's abdomen. It knocked the air right out of that poor man. Lori was in shock. She chided Tommy and immediately began apologizing to the doctor. She could not believe what had just happened. Could it get any worse?

The doctor was furious. His face went from ashen to stop-sign red in a nanosecond. He began to scold Lori for not having control of her child. He talked about discipline and a litany of other parental shortcomings. Lori felt a flood of emotions. It was like Susan was standing in front of her again calling him a little monster. She tried to explain that Tommy was just afraid and was not usually a discipline problem. However, it all fell on deaf ears.

Honestly, she was sort of glad Tommy landed the kick in that moment. She knew that was not the right thing to feel, but the man was a jerk. Tommy did not react to any of the other doctors that way. He still did not like coming, but at least they took the time to help reassure him and make the visit as pleasant as possible.

On the way home, she began replaying the scene in her mind. *I am a bad mom*, she thought. *Why isn't Tommy talking yet? Should I be forcing him to tolerate the vacuum cleaner? What am I doing wrong? Is it because of the pregnancy or troubled birth hours? It has to be my fault. Is something wrong with Tommy?* The words of the doctor floated through her mind over and over, leaving her feeling like a complete failure. She replayed the words of Susan telling her Tommy was out of control and a little monster, like a broken record that keeps skipping.

She felt angry and sad that it was this hard. Her life had changed so much since Tommy was born. She felt so sorry for Tommy. He can't tell her, or anyone for that matter, when he is afraid, or even why he is afraid. The first year of his life had been pretty typical. Except for food and sleep issues, it was all she had anticipated. It was so different now.

She had been so excited for parenthood, but her experience did not resemble anything like what other moms went through or stories she had been told. She had to clip his nails and cut his hair during his sleep. She could not vacuum or blow-dry her hair while he was awake, or he would scream bloody murder. It was like life was a torture chamber for her son, and they were stuck inside this little house of horrors that did not seem to bother any other inhabitants but them. She felt overwhelmed and guilty for feeling unsatisfied or overburdened.

She had let her son down. A good mother would never feel like her child was too difficult. She would never feel ashamed of her child's behavior when they clearly couldn't help it. It felt like she was losing her son, but he was right there with her. What was she feeling? She wanted so desperately to connect and talk with Tommy like she saw other mothers do with their three year olds. She looked at his adorable little face in the back seat on the way home, as tears ran down her cheeks. She loved him so much!

In the past, she had asked about his development with other pediatricians. They all told her the same thing, "Just give it time." Sometimes boys develop a little later. Tommy used words, potty trained, attended preschool, and looked typical *physically. She made a decision to call the local hospital tomorrow and schedule a speech evaluation on her own. She was not willing to wait and see any longer. She decided to talk it over with Mike when he got home.*

Mike got home sometime after 7:00 and appeared very tired. Lori tried to hide her emotions but the tears began to flow. She told him about the trip to the doctor's office and the karate kick that nearly laid the Grinch out. Mike snickered. He told her he thought Tommy was fine, but if it would make her feel better and ease her worry, then he would agree to the speech evaluation. She told him she would call first thing in the morning.

She tried explaining her feelings to Mike, including the guilt she often felt, but he did not understand. Lori felt like it was her responsibility to teach Tommy, as he grew. She felt like a failure because he wasn't developing like other kids his age. She wondered if Mike didn't feel the guilt because he doesn't see the delays, or because he is not the one responsible for teaching him. She is the primary caregiver, not Mike. If Tommy is behind, somehow it is her fault, at least in her mind.

Lori cried herself to sleep silently. She felt very alone. She felt like both an advocate and an accuser of her son, the one she adored. Maybe a fresh set of eyes, she thought. Lord, she prayed, please send us help. A speech teacher can teach him how to talk and everything will get better…

I can remember, just like we witness here with Lori, feeling very torn over my emotions that I experienced in response to negative situations surrounding my son's behavior. I did not like the stares, perceived judgment, real judgment, difficulty, exhaustion, tantrums, and other situations I had to endure surrounding my son. I felt so guilty. I knew instinctively he could not help most of it. I just did not know why. I didn't know what he could or could not help. It made parenting go from joyous to treacherous. There was definitely still joy at times, of course, but it was also really hard. Those toddler years were difficult due to typical toddler issues, but also, because of not so typical reasons. When you add those together, look out!

We are long past the toddler years, and the joy and love I have for my son is still overwhelming. My son has never been and never will be a source of grief or loss. The grief or feelings of loss occurs only when I am forced to make him try to fit into a society that measures success by expected norms such as forming friendships, sports, grades, popularity, college, career, marriage, etc. He can't compete when measured against the average, because he doesn't have all the tools available to the average.

You may be reading this book and have a son or daughter that is gifted academically or struggles socially. Whatever the case, this book is not intended to compare levels of functioning among children. It is to validate emotional responses and help you separate personal expectations from society's expectations. We know what the world expects of our kids, and we know what our kids can do. When our kids are unable to measure up or fit in, we feel it. Learning to set your own expectations based on personal ability may help you achieve healthier adapting, since you will be developing your own definition of success and happiness. We will talk more about this later.

We are all aware of how society measures success. Like it or not, most of us tend to use those same measures to evaluate our own lives and the lives of others. It is my hope and belief that you love your child unconditionally, just as I love mine. In spite of that truth, maybe you also have struggled or continue to struggle with the loss of "normal" and the emotionally challenging circumstances that you encounter.

Do you remember the old animated Christmas movie about Rudolf the red-nosed reindeer and the island of misfits? The story was simple. The toys ended up there because they were different from the other toys, or because they had broken parts, etc. The remedy was to fix them, so they could be placed back with the other toys and be acceptable as Christmas gifts for children.

In the early years, just after my son's diagnosis, I felt like I was swimming upstream to try to fix my child, so he would be deemed acceptable by society and fit into the agreed upon norms. Early interventions such as ABA (Applied Behavioral Analysis) showed promise for greatly improved outcomes. But the window was narrow and time was of the essence. I did not want him stuck on the island of misfits!

I could care less if he was popular. I just wanted him to fit somewhere! I wanted him to have friends and to grow up to be an independent adult! It was so much pressure! My intent was not to put pressure on him but to spare him from grief or pain. Unfortunately, I did put pressure on him, and looking back, I realize, sometimes it was too much pressure and maybe for the wrong reasons. It is a humbling and sad admission but honest nonetheless.

In his later teens, I recall feeling guilty for all the pressure I placed on him to conform. Some conformity is necessary but not all. I felt guilty for always trying to fix him. I wondered how he felt after seeing professionals for years, always focused on what he needed to "work on." There is a balance, and admittedly, I struggled to find it for years, failing miserably at points along the way.

Now that he is an adult and we are many years post diagnosis, I would argue he is acceptable with all of his uniqueness. He embodies qualities that are not measured by our society's norms. I have come to celebrate all of who he is and work diligently to mimic his kindness and love for others. He still lives with us in his "apartment." He is mostly independent and drives to limited locations which do not involve heavy traffic. He takes a carpentry class every semester that his father attends with him. He volunteers in my practice for non-client based job duties each Friday afternoon. He completes work each day that we call "college" work, to keep his mind busy and promote independence. I could not be more proud of the man he has become. By our definition and his, he is successful and happy!

I am not implying that we should just love them and not work with our children to help them reach their full potential academically and otherwise, because we definitely SHOULD. I believe my son continues to reach his potential and beyond. How we measure success and define normal may need to look very different than society's definition, though. I believe we, and our children, regardless of functioning level, can learn to strive for balance and work to achieve success and happiness. We do not have to meet the definition of "normal" to achieve success. Success may be moving out and living independently one day or it may not. It has to be individually assessed based on quality, desires, and ability.

Our emotional reactions to the loss of "normal" can interfere with our ability to have that quality of life. I think it becomes easier with age and experience, but the years in between need not be lost because we lack knowledge. I hope reading about A-typical Cyclic Grief (ACG) will generate conversations allowing you to talk about how you feel without fear of judgment. This topic should not be a source of shame. ACG can affect communication, parenting, family balance, marriage, work, and overall emotional health.

The grief you feel related to your child's disability has nothing to do with your love or loyalty as a parent. Sometimes tantrums and challenging behaviors place higher demands on you as a parent. Again, the negative feelings you may have are not aimed at your child. Rather, they are in response to the disability your child has, because it creates more difficult circumstances.

When I first developed the model, I thought I would attempt to get a journal article published inside a professional journal in my field. To my delight, two of the editors really liked the article and understood the importance of the topic. They were favorable to moving forward if I was willing to do some additional work. The third editor's comments blew me away.

The thing that stood out to me was her position on grief and disability. She was overly critical of the idea that people grieve over their child's disability. She went on to say that she believed parents would be insulted by someone saying his/her child was a source of grief.

It was glaringly obvious she did NOT understand the model or the grief we experience. However, I realized that she was mirroring society's obsession of only focusing on ability and positivity, largely ignoring the grief or challenges faced by many of us every day. It felt as if she were shaming me for expressing grief related to my son's disability.

If you have a child with a disability, then you know the

grief is not because of your child. It is because of the challenges and losses you and your child will experience because of the disability. If it is okay to celebrate the wins, it is also okay to grieve the losses. Why should our grief have to be hidden or shamed into silence?

Learning to talk about it and deal with it in healthier ways will help us adapt to our personalized normal. It will also give others insight into our A-typical journey and hopefully build bridges instead of fences. Lori is experiencing a lot of shame and guilt in isolation. Think about your own reactions to your child's disability along the way.

Challenge Questions:

1. **Think about a time when you felt embarrassed by your child's behavior or stares from others because of your child's behavior. What emotions did you experience?**

2. **What about your own thoughts? Have you had thoughts that made you feel guilty as a parent? Maybe these thoughts occurred because things are hard or haven't turned out the way you expected?**

Remember: Our children are NOT our source of grief! The grief is caused by the loss of "normal" and all it represents.

Chapter 5: The Point of Impact

He reached across the little table and lightly touched the toy animal. The table and chair were both toddler size. Lori was beside him on her knees. "Good job! Now, point to the fruit," said the speech pathologist named Teresa. It took an act of God to talk Teresa into letting her come into the sessions. She was so grateful to be given the chance. Teresa had reiterated that children do not do as well when their parents are in the room with them. However, Lori promised her that she and Tommy would be different. She needed to learn how to help her son.

She recalled the day they came in for testing. Tommy was three years and eight months old at the time. He tested in the year and a half to two year old range for what he understood and in the six month old range for what he could express. No wonder he pulled me everywhere to show me what he needed or wanted, Lori thought to herself. He really did not have the words. She felt so guilty that she had not brought him sooner.

Developmentally delayed is the label they gave Tommy when he started therapy. Okay, Lori thought, a delay means he will catch up. He just got off to a slow start. They had been coming to speech and occupational therapy for close to seven months now. Lori would watch and learn at every session, which occurred twice a week. She would practice whatever they were working on in therapy at home in between sessions. Tommy's progress was remarkable. Once, he had gained close to a year in a matter of months in his receptive language skills. Lori knew it was an answer to prayers.

She had always been a person of faith, although there were several times, during her teen years, when you would have never known it. She spent many of those years trying to overcome her own insecurities, figuring out who she was as a person, and making her own decisions, some good and some bad.

After reaching her mid twenties, she had left all that behind. She grew up, or so she thought. She became very active in a local church. She eventually taught teenage girls in a Sunday school class. She graduated from a Christian school, so she was versed in the bible. She realized later in her older years that there was a difference between knowing the Bible, and recognizing what Christ had done for her as an act of redeeming love. The personal acceptance of this great truth and love changed her down in her core. She tried very hard to be a good Christian and do the right thing.

She did not consider herself better than anyone but could be judgmental at times, if she was being honest. She had always been independent and didn't like being told what to think or believe. She assumed others didn't either. So, she didn't push her faith on others because she believed that each person had to make their own decisions, just like she had done. She prided herself on respecting the rights of others and accepting people, same or different. It was more like she believed God would make everything right in her own life if she did her part.

Her faith grew as she became a mother and witnessed the awe of birth. The first breath and cry of her child only confirmed her beliefs. It was like she had a different perspective of the love for a child that God feels for His children. Although lately, her faith was being stretched like a rubber band. She was praying constantly for Tommy to be okay. She prayed for God to heal him if something was wrong. She prayed and prayed and prayed.

She heard Teresa say, great job again. Tommy was sorting a pile of various items into their own categories. When he got distracted or tired, he would pick up an item and begin to hold it up to his eye and move it back and forth. He looked as if he were studying it to memorize every little detail. He would often repeat phrases or words over and over. Sometimes the words sounded like a distorted version of the original.

Teresa once asked her where he got his British accent. Tommy didn't just mimic words or phrases, but also accents and tone of voice, Lori explained. He had been watching a video of a British man teaching the ABC's and could parrot him to a tee. One day, Lori asked Teresa if she would give her some literature on developmental delays. She told her that she didn't understand some of the other odd behaviors and was hoping to learn more. Teresa hesitated. When she started to speak, the look on her face scared Lori.

Teresa explained to Lori that she was not allowed to diagnose a child. She said she had been told not to tell Lori what *she and several others suspected. Lori was confused. What do you mean? What do you suspect? She told her that Tommy's delays and behaviors look more like a pervasive developmental disorder. "What is that?" Lori asked. Teresa explained further and pulled out literature for her to take home and read. She again told her that she could not make a diagnosis.*

Tommy was tired and ready to go. They loaded into the car and headed home. Lori felt like a ton of bricks were sitting on her shoulders. She could not wait to get home and read the information once she got Tommy settled. They got home around 3:00 p.m., and she put on one of Tommy's favorite videos. He was completely engrossed. She rounded up the information and sat down to read. Oh- my-gosh, she couldn't believe what she was reading. It described her son. It was like she had been a dark tunnel and was finally getting close to the other side. She could see the light shining into the darkness for the first time. Confusion and suspicion were giving way to disbelief and fear.

Pervasive Developmental Disorder was an umbrella type category for several different conditions, Autistic Disorder and Asperger Syndrome being two of them. Shock waves moved into every nerve ending of her body. Could this be true, she wondered. No way! Teresa had told her she could not diagnose. Maybe she just wanted her to read this because it was similar. Lori was at a loss. She didn't even know what it would mean if Tommy was autistic. She heard Mike pulling in from work.

Mike came in the front door and immediately asked Lori what was wrong. She could not hide her fear. She showed him the information, and he immediately dismissed it, saying it was one person's suspicion. "I won't believe it until a doctor says it is true," he stated. He was angry. Mike said, "Who does she think she is anyway, saying something like that to you." "Look at him." "There is nothing wrong with him." "He is just a little behind, but he is catching up, right?" Mike slammed the door, heading back outside.

He came back in later asking what she had been doing all day besides wasting time reading that junk. He was in a mood. She could tell. He found a leaf in the backseat of the car, and went into a rage, accusing her of sleeping with someone in the backseat. She could not believe it. He took her clothes and started sniffing them for traces of cologne. He ranted about a car driving down the street he had not seen before, making accusations that it was her boyfriend. He called her names, belittling her character. All the while, Tommy was lost in his video, oblivious.

She locked herself in the bathroom, crying and desperate, wondering how much more she could take. She was innocent and Mike seemed to be getting worse, almost delusional at times. She had to keep it together, she chided herself. Tommy needs you. Her mind drifted back to their young years together when Mike talked about his own father and how he accused his mother of cheating all the time and was abusive towards her. She remembered his words, "I'll never do that to my wife." He is doing it to his wife, she thought. History repeats itself. She felt trapped and overwhelmed. What if Mike keeps getting worse? What if Tommy is autistic? Can I raise him alone? Fear and sadness gripped her heart. She sat in silence.

She finally came out of the bathroom, and Mike had calmed down. Tommy was staring at a toy in an odd fashion, lost in his own world. Mike apologized but without sincerity. He asked what she had made for dinner. She played along, as if all were fine, and got dinner on the table. She knew deep down the accusations and verbal abuse would happen again. She just didn't know when. She did know it would be sooner than later.

The next day, she called her insurance company to ask about getting Tommy tested and inquired about whether or not it would be covered. She told the lady she needed to have him tested for autism. The lady was very nice and helpful. She helped Lori find a doctor several hours away that specialized in autism and even made the appointment for her. Mike said he would go to the appointment with her.

A couple of months later, the day had arrived. They drove the three hours and arrived a little early to the appointment. The doctor was very nice and had been observing them out in the lobby before they came into her office. She saw Tommy for a follow up visit two weeks later. At the final visit, she told Lori and Mike that Tommy had Pervasive Developmental

Disorder Not Otherwise Specified. The terminology was still Greek to them. The doctor explained that Tommy had a higher functioning form of Autism that fell into the broader category of Pervasive Developmental Disorder Not Otherwise Specified. It was still a diagnosis of Autism, mild or not.

The doctor was very positive, but they knew it was not good news. Mike was visibly shaken. Lori's worst fears and years of worry all became validated in that one moment. She felt both relief to know what they were dealing with and disbelief that it was true. Her mind was reeling with thoughts and her heart a raging sea of emotions.

Mike was quite, lost in his own emotions. He scooped Tommy up and said, "come on little buddy." Lori felt as if she had just been hit by a train, some invisible point of impact that left her bleeding on the inside. What happens next? What about Tommy? What does this mean? She could barely take in all that the doctor said. Please God.....

Sometimes it feels like yesterday and other times it feels like several lifetimes ago. The clarity is still the same. The day I learned my beautiful little blonde headed boy had autism is forevermore burned into my memory. I didn't even know what autism was, except I was pretty sure it wasn't good. I read everything I could get my hands on and vowed to do everything to help my little man. My point of impact brought out the fight in me.

Can you remember your point of impact? The day you learned that your child had a disability. My son, like Tommy, was around the age of four when he was diagnosed. I was a stay-at-home mom and determined to do whatever it took for him to catch up and beat the odds.

The point of impact can happen at anytime along the lifespan, even as early as in the womb. In one of my presentations on A-typical Cyclic Grief, I met a couple who had a daughter that had suffered a traumatic brain injury in a car accident at the age of 19. After hearing my presentation, they asked to speak with me. We talked for a long time, and I learned that one of their difficulties was trying to psychologically adapt to their new normal after having so many years of "normal". Their daughter had not been born with a disability but rather developed a disability due to injury later in life. She was in her first year of college when the accident occurred. She was a bright and pretty girl with a promising future, the mom shared.

They admitted that they often responded to her in the same ways they had prior to the disability and would become frustrated with her progress. For years, they had believed she would fully recover. To them, that meant she would get back to "normal". Life would be like it was before the accident. They had been chasing "normal" for a long time when I met them. They told me that understanding how A-typical Cyclic Grief had kept them in a repeat cycle finally gave them a new awareness and hope to do something different. Trying to recover "normal" was the wrong goal.

Adapting to their new normal was a process for both their daughter and for them. They loved her very much and they were proud of the progress she had made, but also recognized that they needed to readjust their expectations based on their new normal, not the old one. She was still a pretty girl with a promising future, just a different future with new definitions of promise.

On a different occasion, another mom introduced me to her infectiously charming son with Down Syndrome. She told me her point of impact was when her son was still in the womb. She talked about the grief process and also how learning about the disability prior to birth helped her learn more about the disability and prepare for the psychological changes of normal. She did not imply that she averted the grief process, because she knew prior to birth of his condition. Rather, her on ramp to A-typical Cyclic Grief was at the start of life. Perhaps denial was briefer as well due to the visibility of the disability at birth.

The types of disability are many, but the one common factor we all have is a point of impact. The minute you learned that your child and yourself would face struggles or limitations caused by loss of "normal", you had your moment of impact. It is important to note that the level of grief is often directly related to the degree of limitations imposed by the disability.

For example, a learning disorder affecting Math or

Reading can certainly pose challenges and limitations for children and their parents. However, they do not typically make the child stand out in ways that draw unwanted attention or limit everyday functioning in society. The disability or disorder shows up academically, but is usually camouflaged in most, if not all, other areas of life. These parents may experience grief if the child is unable to attend college or maybe even graduate with a diploma. But they may still be able to marry, have children, and hold down a job. So, the loss of "normal" may be limited to one area of life. Nonetheless, grief is still experienced and can be painful for both the child and the parent.

In contrast, a child with Down Syndrome, Intellectual Disability, or Autism Spectrum Disorder, may face limitations academically, verbally, behaviorally, socially, and intellectually causing multiple areas of life to be impacted. The unmet milestones and grief occurrences will be more frequent and occur repeatedly over the lifespan.

Grief is grief and this is not meant to compare disabilities. However, the number of times you cycle through the emotions described in the model and the degree to which you feel the grief is dependent on how much the disability impacts your life. We are all impacted at some level when the loss of an expected norm occurs. That is what makes ACG common to all of us, but the degree will vary depending on individualized circumstances.

Frequently, people are unprepared emotionally and mentally to fully process the realization of a diagnosis that confirms a life changing disability. Even if we as parents suspect something may be wrong, as in Lori's case, to hear the diagnosis from a professional can be emotionally difficult. It can feel like an invisible punch in the gut that knocks the wind out of you. The point of impact is the on-ramp to A-typical Cyclic Grief. The next stop is denial. Take some time to read through and answer the challenge questions on the next page. Try to remember the day you learned of your own child's diagnosis and how you felt during that time.

Challenge Questions:

1. Do you remember the first time you learned of your child's diagnosis?

2. What emotions did you feel?

3. What thoughts ran through your mind?

4. Did you feel shocked? Dismayed? What about unprepared for the challenge?

5. Did it bring out a fight or flight response in you?

Remember: The point of impact is the on-ramp and adapting is the off-ramp! We don't have to stay stuck in the cycle. Yes, our lives have changed, but we are created to adapt to change!

Chapter 6: The Slippery Slope of Denial

Mike was somber on the ride home. Lori tried talking to him about the doctor's comments, but he was not open to talking. She knew he was trying to deal with his own feelings and maybe for the first time, accept that something was wrong. Tommy is not developing normally. He is not a "normal" little boy. He is autistic. No matter how "high functioning" the doctor describes him, she also made sure to say there was no cure and that he would be in therapy for a long time to come.

She did tell us not to limit him, and encouraged us to visit a local autism center so we could see the difference between Tommy and other kids who were more severely impaired. No cure. The thought made her sick. It felt like a bad dream. Hopeless! How can this be? Why my son?

No! I'm not giving up that easy, she thought! She blurted out to Mike, God is bigger, and he is going to make Tommy better. She rejected the limitations and vowed to beat the diagnosis. It's only a name, a label, it doesn't predict the future. Mike did not say anything. He was silent. Tommy was staring out the window as they traveled, taking in all the details.

Deep down inside, she knew the diagnosis fit, but she still argued that he could not be autistic. How could they not have known? She went back and forth in her mind. She believed it, and then she didn't. Mike finally spoke up and said, "I'm not sure about the diagnosis, but if he is special, then so be it." As time passed, Mike began to distance himself more from Tommy. He struggled to relate to him. It was as if the diagnosis somehow changed the way Mike saw him. He still loved him but more in a caretaker sort of way, rather than in a father/son sort of way. Lori did the opposite. Her life became all about Tommy. She went to therapy 4 to 5 times a week with him to learn and practice at home.

Lori would encourage Mike to teach him things or spend time with him, but he always made excuses saying he was too busy or that Tommy should spend time with her, because she was the only one who understood him. She remembers telling her parents about the diagnosis and her father's denial. He refused to believe it. He said no one would convince him that Tommy wasn't smart. It might take him a little longer, but he is doing better every day. "He is going to catch up and grow out of this, you mark my words," he would say. Lori looked up to her father, so his words fueled her greatest hopes and prayers, that he would grow out of it. He would be normal or at least close.

She dug in deeper to therapy and really became somewhat obsessed with his progress. It was therapy every day, all day. She made it fun, and most of the time Tommy did not even know it was therapy. To him, it was play. Mike's accusations and moodiness increasingly got worse. His mood swings were obvious. She never knew what to expect and found herself tip-toeing around him all the time. It was like walking on eggshells. She loved him because he was Tommy's father, but it was becoming more and more difficult to feel love for him in other ways because of how he treated her.

She was throwing a ball to Tommy, while he was jumping on the bed, because the bi-lateral movements were important for his development and focusing. She set the bed up in a way that he could not fall off. They did not have a trampoline, so this would have to do. She glanced up at his preschool graduation picture and recalled the day she shared the news of his diagnosis with his teacher and the director. Both of them did not believe it. They told Lori how smart he was and how they knew he would be just fine in time. Again, it had been just what she wanted to hear. His teacher said she worried more about other children than Tommy, because she felt like he was going to grow up to be a fine young man.

Tommy was very smart. He knew his alphabet phonetically by the age of three, and was decoding words by the age of four. He could do so many things, some things more advanced than other kids his age. He was a loving child and enjoyed getting hugs and tickles. He bonded with his teachers and did not fit the stereotypical picture of someone with autism. Questioning the diagnosis became a familiar dance for Lori. She would witness his odd behaviors and limited speech, confirming the diagnosis. Others would tell her how typical some of his behaviors were and how they knew a friend whose child didn't talk until the age of four. Lori found their words so comforting

48

because they fed her deep desire to believe that Tommy would be fine.

Lori was sure they would beat this. She believed God was healing him every day. Even his teachers, her friends, and her parents all saw the progress. Tommy will be fine. He will grow up to live a "normal" life...

The tears were rolling down her cheeks as she hid just out of sight from him. It was his first day of kindergarten and he sat there with his little hands covering his face. All alone without her, panic was setting in; it took all of her strength not to burst into the room and scoop him up, never to return. It was like she had been in some alternate universe where Tommy appeared almost "normal" over the past year. Now, the contrast between him and his chattering classmates was like bitter grapes.

He looked so differently when compared to other kids his age. They were all talking to each other, several of them attempting to talk to him. Tommy cannot hold a typical conversation. He has made a lot of progress, but he still can't keep up to the level of the other children. She wasn't even sure if he would ask to go to the restroom or even knew he could ask to go to the restroom. She expressed her concerns a few minutes ago, and the teacher had assured her that all parents feel this way the first day of kindergarten. She had a hard time believing that! She felt like she was dropping him off on a curb in China, then speeding away, knowing he can only speak English and will be lost and scared. What kind of mother does that?

He looked so scared and fragile. What is she doing? She feels like she is betraying him. She left him vulnerable without protection. She called her friend who encouraged her to let Tommy have a chance to prove what he can do. She went to her friend's house and cried her way through several cups of coffee. She thought 3:00 would never come.

Finally, it was time. She went inside to pick him up, and he looked happy to see her. The teacher said he had a good day and the children were nice to him. Tommy said nothing. She tried to get him to tell her what he had done in school or name one of the kids in his class, but he was zoned out. Lori could not describe all the emotions floating inside her head. How could he

49

look so normal at times and so impaired at others? Was she not seeing the limitations because she didn't want to? All she knew was that he had made it through his first day of Kindergarten and that was something to celebrate.

A few months into the school year, she felt better about dropping him off and realized it was good for him to be on his own. She remembered the day he even got in trouble. She thought to herself, "that's normal, right?" At least it seemed normal, until she learned what he got in trouble for that day when she was picking him up. The teacher told her he got his hand slapped for spitting water. Lori was shocked, because that did not sound like Tommy. After listening to the teacher explain, she realized he had been spraying it out of his mouth in order to watch the water in the air. This was something he sometimes did at home.

It was not an act of defiance, but more a self-stimming behavior, as they called it in the world of autism. Self-stimming is a term used to describe behaviors that children use to soothe or calm themselves in a repetitive fashion. Lori was told by the professionals, that it is common in children with autism.

She felt the strangest need to protect and defend him. She knew spitting was not acceptable, even if it was for self stimulation. But was it okay to punish him for it? She allowed Tommy to do it at home in the bathroom sink or outside. There were so few things he really enjoyed, so she did not want to take away the things he did. The older he got, the more she found herself trying to make up for all the things he was missing out on. He hardly ever asked for a toy, so when he did, she wanted to buy it for him. He worked so hard in therapy all the time. She just wanted him to be happy. It was so hard to figure out when to discipline him or when he couldn't help it.

Overall, he was a good boy. The tantrums could be hurricane force, but he usually didn't ask for much. In fact, it was hard to explain. In many ways, he was far less demanding than other kids, but in other ways, he was far more demanding. She didn't want him to be spoiled, but she also didn't want him to always be on the fringes doing his own thing. It was a tightrope to walk. She continued to pray, but her rubber band of faith was *being stretched to the limits.*

She seemed to be struggling with everything these days. She has lost confidence in her marriage, her ability to parent, her faith, and in finding hope. It will all get better, she chided herself for doubting. This will be the hardest year, but once he finishes Kindergarten, it will get easier. Mike will see that he will be fine. He will start spending more time with him. Mike will get better. This has just been a tough few years for all of us....

Lori knows Tommy has autism, yet she still believes he will beat it and struggles to see his limitations. This may seem like a no brainer and Lori is just being unrealistic, but is it a no brainer? I can relate and have even resembled Lori at times. What about you? Mike seemed to distance himself to deal with the diagnosis. Perhaps he could believe everything would be fine if he was not faced with the limitations.

Lori had several people in her life supporting her need to believe that Tommy would be "normal". In her case, it did not stop her from seeking treatment, however, in some cases it can. Hearing the diagnosis for the first time is an emotional experience. Just like the unexpected death of a loved one can trigger an emotional response of denial, so can the unexpected loss of "normal".

In disabilities that are visible, denial usually does not last as long, because it is more tangible. The disability can be seen, making it more difficult to deny. Denial can be as brief as a short period of shock or dismay. In less visible disabilities, people can cycle in and out of denial for years.

Denial, at times, can be a psychological cushion which protects people from the full impact of the devastating emotional trauma. This is true in a sudden unexpected death, for example. People will talk about feeling surreal as if they are in a dream. They report waking up believing everything has been a dream or just feeling numb like an out of body experience. If you have ever lost someone close to you suddenly, perhaps you can relate to this experience.

Denial is not all bad. It usually resolves itself naturally, in the case of death, because it is virtually impossible to deny the absence of your loved one for an extended period of time. Eventually denial comes to an end. Death is tangible. The denial stage in A-typical Cyclic Grief can be a bit more complicated making it sometimes difficult to recognize as part of the grief process.

I remember the months following my son's diagnosis and the see-saw of thoughts I battled daily. Can this really be happening, I thought? Part of me felt relief and the other felt complete devastation. I remember questioning the diagnosis, because he looked so "normal". I questioned the diagnosis because he was so young. I questioned the diagnosis because it didn't fit with *Rain Man*, a movie I had watched about an autistic man.

It was like my mind was always searching subconsciously to prove the diagnosis was wrong. I wanted my son to be okay so desperately that I welcomed any little thing that would support my hope. I also experienced family members who denied the diagnosis for their own reasons, but I certainly welcomed the safety in numbers they offered. If they think it's wrong, then maybe the diagnosis really is wrong.

When he would stare at a stick for an hour or recite movie lines over and over, I would feel relief to know why. The relief was quickly overshadowed by devastation that my beautiful little boy would be permanently affected for the rest of his life. The doctor was very nice and encouraging about the future, but it did not take away the sting of the diagnosis and what it represented. My experience is not unique.

Feelings of disbelief and shock can leave you emotionally unable or unwilling to accept the diagnosis as valid or permanent. At this stage of grief, it is not uncommon for you to seek a second opinion or totally reject the information as true. Denial will generate thoughts like, "That is not possible!!" "Well, that doesn't mean anything. He or she will be just fine!" "I would have noticed before now!" "That doctor was a quack!" I'm sure you could add a few thoughts to this list as well.

Why do we have such strong reactions to a diagnosis? It signifies the loss of "NORMAL!" It is the loss of our dreams, expectations, and the familiar script you thought would be yours and your child's. Think about Lori and Mike's life before having Tommy. They did not experience disability. They expected their child would be "normal", just like them and face "normal" everyday problems.

Our culture is really big on trendy phrases these days like "what is normal anyway" or "normal is just a myth". Is it? I think in terms of traditional views in our society "normal" IS ever changing. For example, the traditional definition of family that used to be the norm has definitely changed. There is a new "normal" or new definition of family. The blended family or nontraditional forms of family seem to represent the new "normal" and is much more widely accepted than in years past.

There are many other examples we could use, however, we are not talking about traditional views that shape the norms in this context of "normal". People can make different life choices; live in blended families, and live minimalistic life styles, etc and still go on to lead functional lives. Having a disability is not choosing to live outside of the norm. *It is losing the ability to live inside the norm. It is not a choice, rather it is a loss.* We are talking about "normal" versus abnormal, ability versus limitations, and meeting milestones versus missing milestones.

What does "Normal" really mean? Does it exist? How is it defined by our Society? According to Merriam-Webster: Normal is defined as: 2.(a) According with, constituting, or not deviating from a norm, rule, or principle (b) conforming to a type, standard, or regular pattern 4. (a) of, relating to, or characterized by average intelligence or development. (b) free from mental disorder: sane. I encourage you to look it up for yourself. We do define and expect "normal".

As you can see, "normal" is partially defined by conformity. People who choose not to conform to the standards, rules, or patterns would be considered outside the norm by choice. They can, at any time, choose to conform and find themselves within the norm. People who fall outside of "normal" because they do not have average intelligence or development, can't conform. It's not a choice they are making to live counter to cultural norms. If you are living outside the "normal" limits due to your child's developmental disability, you clearly understand the distinction.

If our culture in the United States is made up of all types of diversity, is there really a collective standard? YES! Everything we know and understand is based on societal norms! Not to be too technical, but let's look at the definition of a norm.

According to Merriam-Webster: A Norm is defined as: 1. an authoritative standard 3. Average as; (a) a set standard of development or achievement usually derived from the average or median achievement of a large group (b) a pattern or trait taken to be typical in the behavior of a social group (c) a widespread or usual practice, procedure, or custom.

When a diagnosis of a developmental disability is given, it means the familiar is gone in one swift swoop! We have actually lost the familiar script we all plan to experience as we move through life. It has all changed. We have lost the shared commonality with the majority in our culture. The script has been changed, rewritten, and we are not familiar with the new script. We have lost the ability to conform to the expected norms of our culture.

This deep loss and substantial change can cause you to reject the information or diagnosis as true in this first stage of denial. Either "it's not true" or "we will get back what we lost" are common first responses.

It is important to recognize and point out four specific Denial Dangers that can occur in A-typical Cyclic Grief. These dangers can have lasting impacts and need to be dealt with quickly. Denying a disability will not make the disability go away.

Denial Dangers:
1) Denial can be encouraged by others, because the diagnosis may be less visible in some forms of disability and explained away by well meaning family members. This can reinforce your feelings of denial.
2) Denial can last much longer in certain situations because children, especially young children, will grow and mature, which can also support the idea that they will grow out of it. In other words, you may believe that the doctor was

wrong because your child would not be able to do these things if the diagnosis were correct.

3) Denial can also contribute to the rejection of beneficial, and sometimes necessary, interventions for your child impacted by the disability. You may not seek out appropriate treatment if you remain in a state of denial. This is especially critical in situations where early intervention is important to improved outcomes.

4) Denial can cause you to react incorrectly to your child, when or if they do not meet the expectations of "normal". If you deny the existence of a disability that is affecting your child's ability to perform or function within the predicted norms, you may unintentionally cause them emotional pain and create feelings of worthlessness or helplessness. Think about it. If you had diabetes and someone punished you every time your sugar dropped, you would eventually begin to feel helpless, defeated, worthless, and bitter.

Denying some information can be good, but caution and good judgment is necessary.

Nicole's story

Nicole approached me after hearing one of my presentations on ACG. She told me her story, and asked if I would share her story with others, so that they would not have to endure the same suffering. She told me that the psychiatrist who diagnosed her son with autism also provided psychotherapy to her to help her cope with the diagnosis and disability. In one of her sessions, he told her that her son's autism was a result of her past sins. She talked about years of guilt and confusion she had to endure on her own.

Her experience is a perfect example of information that should have been rejected! This is an extreme example; however, I have heard stories from countless people about hurtful statements. Sometimes those statements even came from professionals. I recall a mom and dad I met at our local autism support group who talked about their diagnosis experience. They said the doctor told them to institutionalize their son, because he would never be able to do anything for himself. Their son was only four at the time. They rejected that information and raised their son at home. He still lives at home and goes to a day program that he enjoys through the week. He can do many things.

In both cases, the information was the opinion of one person and warranted a second opinion. Nicole knew her doctor's statements could not be true; even so, it still haunted her for years. When it comes to denial, we have to use good judgment in what we reject and what we accept.

In case you are wondering, the doctor Nichole described is no longer practicing. Her son was an adult when I met her, and the doctor had long since retired when she shared her story. She is fully confident that her son's autism is not her fault.

You may have your own horror story, or perhaps like me, you had a pleasant and encouraging doctor. Either way, knowing what to accept and what to reject can be difficult at times.

Having a child with a disability requires you to make mental and emotional adjustments. It may impact changes in future plans or visions of the future. We plan our lives around the expected norms. In other words, we usually do not plan for a child with a disability, and often times, there is a lack of understanding and emotional support for those of us raising our amazing kids.

We love our children, disability or not, but this road less traveled can be very difficult at times. Take some time to be honest with yourself. Dig deep. Work through the following challenge questions before moving on to the next chapter. We can get through this together.

Challenge Questions:

1. **Where are you in your journey?**

2. **What were your reactions when you first learned of the diagnosis?**

3. Did you or are you currently struggling with accepting a diagnosis for your child?

4. Have others around you caused you to question whether or not your child really has a disability?

5. Have you experienced hurtful words or maybe even fear that has caused you to withdraw from professionals or possibly deny a diagnosis?

6. Are any of the denial dangers getting in the way of seeking out help for your child?

Remember: Your normal may be different from the "normal" you expected, but your life and the life of your child can still be good and happy!

Chapter 7: This Isn't Fair!

She felt a sense of pride as she looked over the progress report Tommy's teacher had sent home. He is doing well and the teachers seem to love him. She is so thankful she made the decision to put Tommy in public school and let him repeat Kindergarten. He has a full time adult (called an aide) that is with him all day to assist with his learning. The private school was unable to offer comparable services, and she believed he really needed the help. She was glad he was doing well for the moment, which is more than she can say for her marriage.

It had been two weeks since Mike moved in with a coworker, a nice couple that offered him a room for a while. It had been a miserable Christmas. Mike's behaviors had gone from unbearable to downright bizarre. It started really going downhill several months ago. He started working odd hours, changing grooming habits, and accused Lori almost daily of being unfaithful to him. He believed the neighbors were talking about him and following him home from work. Lori went from being angry and fed up to being concerned. She told Mike he needed help. She insisted that he see a counselor to deal with his jealousy and paranoia, otherwise she was leaving.

He told her he would go, but nothing changed. Instead, things just got worse. She reflected back on the night two weeks ago when he was yelling at her, and out of nowhere, little Tommy shouted, "Stop hollering!" It was the first time ever that Tommy noticed the arguing. Now as she thought back on the situation, she was both dumbfounded and elated that he had used words in such a meaningful way. She was also sad it was in response to such a bad situation. She recalled looking at Mike, expecting that response from Tommy to jolt him into some realization of his behavior. It did not.

Mike turned his anger towards Tommy. The shock was penetrating and only secondary to the anger that rose up within her. Mike was yelling at Tommy, denying the fact that he was "hollering" and told him he needed to go play. It was one thing to take Mike's yelling and accusations, as long as Tommy was not targeted, but this was a game changer, Lori thought. He had crossed the line! She turned to Mike and told him to get out! It is *over! She told him she would never allow him to do to Tommy what he had done to her.*

Mike was furious and still acting out in bizarre ways. She left to go to her mother's overnight, while Mike got his things and found somewhere to go. He landed at a friend's house that he worked with on the same shift. Two weeks passed and she and Mike had talked several times throughout the time span. Mike agreed to go to counseling again and she encouraged him to take some time to spend with his family and maybe take some time off work. She promised that regardless of their marriage, he would always be a part of Tommy's life. She would never be one of those parents who used the child as leverage or a pawn. But, she also made it clear that he would not treat Tommy badly, and he needed to get help to learn how to deal with whatever was causing him to act aggressively and paranoid.

Mike had come for a visit this past Saturday, and it was a weird day. Tommy refused to go to him. In fact, he acted afraid, and it really upset Mike. Mike was pacing and seemed agitated, causing Lori to worry he might escalate, as he had done several times in the recent past. He did not. Instead, he left in a huff. He tried to call her several times on Sunday, according to her caller ID, but she had been at her brother's house with Tommy. She had awaked with an uneasy feeling Sunday morning, unsure why, but felt that she didn't want to be home alone. She would later learn the reason for her unease.

On Monday morning, she and Tommy were playing and relaxing at home. He was out of school that day, and Lori wanted to spend some quality time with him. She was sitting by the fireplace reading one of Tommy's favorites book to him when the phone rang around 11:00 am. It was Mike's employer. He asked if Mike was there, and she told him that he had been staying with friends. His boss told her he had already spoken with them, and they had not seen Mike since yesterday. He had not shown up for work, so his boss was trying to locate him. He sounded concerned and now Lori felt a sinking feeling in the pit of her gut.

Mike was dependable and was never late for work. He prided himself on being on time and a hard worker. The fact that

*he had not shown up or called was bad, very bad. She called the
people he had been staying with and talked with the wife of the
man Mike worked with. She was very nice and told Lori that
Mike had left to go to the store Sunday evening and never
returned. She said her family had gone to church and was busy
getting ready for the next day, and had not paid much attention to
the fact that Mike was not there.*

*She told her that Mike had given her a letter before he left
for the store, telling her that if anything happened to him, she
was to give the letter to his sister. "What?," Lori thought. Now
bells were really going off in her head. "Did you read the
letter," Lori asked? She said no. Lori asked her to get the letter
and read it to her. It sounded like a goodbye letter. Lori hung up
and immediately contacted Mike's family, hoping he had taken
her advice and decided to go spend some time with them. They
lived in a different state, and the trip would have taken about ten
hours. He should be there by now.*

*One by one, she spoke to each family member. Some said
he had called them the day before and seemed odd, but had said
nothing in particular to set off alarm. He was not there! He did
not leave to spend time with his family. Lori began to fear the
worst. It was a bitterly cold winter day. Where was Mike? She
called the police and reported him missing. It was a call she
never imagined she would make in her lifetime.*

*She did not sleep a wink. She prayed harder than she had
ever prayed before. Please God, protect Mike. Please God, let
him know you love him. Please God, help us find him. Tuesday
morning, around 11:30 a.m., the phone rang. "May I speak to
Mrs. Jones," a deep voice requested. This is she, answered Lori.
It was a detective from a county away. He verified that she was
Mike's wife, and then informed her that Mike had been found in
his truck with three self-inflicted gunshot wounds. He was alive
but barely. She went numb all over. She was in shock.*

*The next hours that followed felt like she was walking in
someone else's life, watching from the outside. It felt surreal. It
was like autopilot had been turned on. Lori had been told Mike
was being flown to the nearest trauma center and, she should
plan to drive directly to the hospital. She called her parents, and*

they went with her and Tommy to the hospital.

Mike arrived before they did and had already been placed in the trauma unit. They checked in at the front desk and were ushered to a private enclosed room within the bigger lobby. She wondered why they were placed in the private room and fought the urge to run out screaming.

It felt like eternity, but finally, a doctor came in to talk with her. He told her that Mike's injuries would be fatal, and had it not been below freezing while he was injured, he would have already bled to death. He had shot himself twice in the chest and once in the head. The bullets to the chest missed all major organs, the doctor explained. The bullets exited the body without causing life- threatening injury. The bullet in his head had exited but left pieces behind and did quite a bit of damage. The doctor said that his body was frozen, and as he warmed up, his brain would swell, and he would eventually die. There was no hope! She was pretty sure she was hearing the doctor's words but not comprehending them.

Lori was ushered into the trauma unit by the doctor to see Mike. The image would be burned into her memory forever. The moment she saw him, she wished she could have erased the image immediately from her mind. The man she saw lying in front of her did not remotely resemble the man she was married to, the father of her son. The injuries had changed his appearance in ways she was unprepared to see.

A wave hit her, causing her to feel like her legs were going to give way and collapse beneath her. Two nurses grabbed an arm on each side, helping her out of the unit. One of the nurses asked her if she was okay, which seemed like a cruel question to ask as she struggled to comprehend the events taking place in front of her eyes. NO! She was not okay! How could this ever be okay?

Mike's body was gradually warmed to the necessary temperature, but he did not die like the doctor predicted. They drained fluid from his brain, and he was placed on life support. The doctor told Lori she needed to decide whether or not to keep him on life support. Her mind was racing and her body was numb. She could not process or take in all that had happened over the past two days or even past few hours. How could she decide between life and death, especially for someone else? Again she prayed, asking God for help. She told the doctor she did not want to make that decision alone. She begged God to take that decision from her.

Mike started breathing on his own before it had to be made. He again had surprised the doctors. Not only did he live after he was warmed to his standard body temperature, but he was able to breathe on his own without life support systems. Thank you God, she whispered.

The days and weeks that followed were like living in some horror film where she was the main character. Tommy, oh poor Tommy! She was again grieving for the living. Mike was alive and dead at the same time. The Mike she knew, Tommy's father, was gone. His body was here but just the shell of him. The incident left him blind and permanently brain injured. Mike was unable to care for himself and was hospitalized for months, then eventually moved to a residential facility.

He had already filed for the divorce prior to the suicide attempt. Lori received the papers soon after he shot himself. He wanted the divorce, and so did she, but now she feels terrible guilt about it. She feels guilty. His family blames her. They said, "He would never have done this to himself if you had not wanted a divorce." They stated these things in front of her to the doctors. Were they right, she wondered? Is this my fault? Blame, guilt, sorrow, shame, and anger all washed over her.

She watched one of the speech therapy sessions with Mike while he was still in the hospital. The therapist was having him point to the fruit, tools, and other categories to test his receptive skills. It was a punch in the gut! She felt like she was in the twilight zone. It was like Tommy had been replaced by Mike in the therapy sessions. It was some twisted form of déjà vu. The irony was so thick and the cruelty of it all seemed too much to comprehend. Why? She couldn't wrap her mind or emotions around it all.

A specialized psychiatrist in the facility approached Lori one afternoon asking to speak with her alone. Up until that point, she had never seen any professional without Mike's family present. She agreed, but Mike's sister- in- law said she was coming too. The doctor told her no. He wanted to speak with Lori alone. Once they were alone, he asked Lori about the days and weeks leading up to Mike's attempt. She told him about the bizarre behavior, paranoia, and jealousy.

The psychiatrist told her that his injuries were violent in nature, and he was thankful that no one else was injured while Mike was in his unstable state of mind. He also told her that he had heard Mike's family, on numerous occasions, say things that indicated it was her fault. His candidness and caring was more than she could take. She burst into tears as he told her that it was not her fault. He assured her that Mike was not well, and there was nothing that she could have done to prevent what had occurred. He also reminded her that lots of people go through divorces and do not injure themselves or others.

She felt so much better after talking with him. She thanked God for sending him to her at a time when she felt so alone. Mike's mother wanted him to be moved to the state where she and his siblings lived, and Lori agreed. She also knew it was time. She had to get back to Tommy. He needed her. He had lost his father. He doesn't need to lose his mother also. Tommy had been staying with her parents and they were all worse for the wear. She packed her bags and headed home from the facility for the last time.

She was an emotional basket case on the drive home. Her mind was swirling with thoughts, mostly scary ones. She was listening to a story on the radio of a woman who had experienced tragedy. The woman posed a question to the listening audience asking if your life has been shattered into a million pieces, maybe it's to feed the multitudes. Lori immediately felt an electric shock in her soul. It's as if she heard God say, "Your shattered life will feed the multitudes one day." She says aloud, "I don't even know five people God, how could I possibly ever feed a multitude", she questions. She dismisses the message and chalks it up to being emotionally spent. She silently continues her journey home.

Before the age of 7, Tommy had witnessed an abusive relationship, been diagnosed with autism, and lost his father. It was more like a death than a survival. There would be no *visitation, no calls on the phone, and no way to explain it to that innocent little boy. She was at a loss. Mike was too impaired to have any relationship with Tommy and Tommy was too impaired to understand why he would not see his daddy anymore. The irony was uncanny. She is now a single parent, she thought, or more like a widower. They were on their own.*

The days, weeks, and months passed, all full of new challenges and fresh waves of anger. She was angry; angry that her son had a disability, angry she could not communicate with him like other mothers, angry that his inability to understand led to outburst and tantrums, angry she was left alone to care for him, angry that everything had to be so hard, angry that nothing had turned out the way in was supposed to, angry at Mike for leaving, angry that life had to be so hard for Tommy, and angry at God!

She didn't understand why God would allow this to happen. She didn't understand why He didn't heal Tommy. She just didn't understand! She felt abandoned by everyone, but mostly by God. She felt cheated and powerless to change it. She was ashamed to tell anyone how she felt, so she kept it all inside. After all, a good mother would not feel angry about her child having a disability. A good Christian would not be angry at God. At least that is what she thought and had been taught to believe.

What am I going to do? How am I going to take care of Tommy on my own? I don't even have a job. Will I be able to work and take care of Tommy? She just wanted it all to be over. Maybe she would wake up to discover it had all been just a horrible nightmare. That is not going to happen, she thought. She would be strong and do whatever it takes.....

Lori has now experienced a secondary loss which added to her anger. You may have experienced a secondary loss as well, such as divorce or an additional child who also has a disability. Whether you have experienced a secondary loss or are feeling anger from the original loss, anger is part of the journey at times. Anger is a common and expected response when you feel as though you or a loved one has been cheated or slighted from a chance at a level playing field. It's not fair! It wasn't supposed to turn out this way!

Once we accept that a disability exists, we become fully aware that it means unexpected challenges and life changes for both you and your child. Our anger can take many forms. Some parents that I have talked to expressed anger towards the pediatrician for not catching it sooner. Or anger because it can't be fixed and it places high demands on their life with no end in sight. They have anger because their son or daughter has to struggle and has been cheated out of a fair chance at life.

I remember shortly after my son was diagnosed, I was so excited to report back to his pediatrician. I honestly believed that the pediatrician would be surprised and happy that I was able to get answers and help for my son.

I was unprepared for the response I was given when I shared my happy news. The doctor told me with a scolding tone, "I could have told you that two years ago, but YOU were in so much denial, it would not have made a difference." WHAT? I was floored! My mind was screaming. He knew two years ago that my son suffered from autism but did not tell me. My son lost two years of intervention because of his assessment of me! Wait? Who was his patient, me or my son? I was angry, devastated, guilty, and confused all at the same time. Needless to say, I changed pediatricians the next day.

Just to be clear, I am not bashing medical professionals. I am so appreciative of the great care my son has received throughout the years, and we have had the privilege to work with some awesome professionals. But, I had to learn early on to make changes when necessary and hold on to the good ones. In the words of Kenny Rogers, "you better know when to hold em', know when to fold em', know when to walk away, and know when to run."

I certainly have experienced strong feelings of anger along the way. I felt angry at times because my son could not just have a "normal" life. Instead of running around to birthday parties, we were marching off to therapies. It did not feel fair! But every time I would look at his sweet young innocent face, I would bury that anger and march on towards making him better. I did not express all the anger I felt. Honestly, I really did not know how to put it all into words. I just felt raw anger that I could not fully blame on any one thing or person. It was a helpless sort of anger.

If I thought blaming the doctor, anyone else, or anything would have made my son better and fixed it all, I would have jumped head long onto that bandwagon. But in my gut, I knew it was just anger from a deep loss that represented change and challenges that I was not prepared for mentally or emotionally. I did not recognize it as a common grief response, because my little boy was alive and physically healthy. No death had occurred, so to me, it was all just selfish negativity.

When we feel overwhelmed by the fear of the unknown, confusion, and helplessness, anger can occur naturally in response. The anger stage of ACG that you will cycle in and out of can be intense at times. It may even make you cynical or resentful, lashing out at the world around you. When people lose a loved one to death, we expect that they will experience anger as part of the grief process. We tend to be more forgiving and understanding of their anger because we recognize it as grief.

When the death of "normal" has occurred, it is not recognized in the same way as a physical death. Yet, we still grieve. If you are new to the journey, you may not recognize your emotions as a grief response. Others around you also may not recognize it as grief. This can lead to your anger or irritability being misunderstood and less tolerated.

Awareness and knowledge will help us recognize our anger as being a part of an expected grief process. That is not to say every time we are angry it is because of our child's disability, but recognizing when anger is caused by grief will help you work through it more effectively. Talk about it with your friends, spouse, and family members. It is a normally occurring emotional reaction to loss.

Because ACG is cyclic, anger can reoccur sometimes frequently, if you are continually reminded of your loss. Each time you encounter situations that highlight and contrast the struggles your child faces compared to non-disabled children, you will probably experience negative emotion. When you feel unfairly judged out in the community or even by family members or friends, it can create new feelings of anger.

When my son was two years old, he thrived on repetitious behavior. If we bought a brown stuffed horse at Wal-Mart on the last trip, we MUST buy another one on the next trip. No diagnosis had been made yet, however, at that age, he was still unable to say his own name, much less mine. It was a sunny day, and we were headed to Wal-Mart to buy groceries. On the previous shopping trip, I had bought him a Cozy Coupe car; you know the red and yellow one made by Little Tykes. You can probably see where this is headed.

He was sitting in the buggy as I was attempting to grocery shop, when we passed by the toy aisle. He immediately began trying to get out of the buggy. I was still clueless about why he was so distressed. I let him out. He ran to the toy aisle and headed straight for the Cozy Coupe Car! Finally, the light bulb came on, and I knew what was coming. Chaos erupted!

He threw the mother of all tantrums. He was thrusting my hand towards the car, throwing himself on the floor, and screaming as if he was being kidnapped. Eventually, I realized that three to four Wal-Mart personnel were circling me with suspicion in their eyes. It occurred to me in that moment that I had no way to prove that I was his mother, except for the fact that he is my facial Twinkie.

As I stood there ready to burst into tears, there she came. She had to have been Mother Teresa or an angel sent by God. The brave soul approached me, while my son was still screaming as if possessed by the dark side. I was honestly waiting for his head to do a 360 degree spin while projectile vomiting. The angel said in a quiet voice, "Does he want a toy dear?" I burst out half crying, "yes ma'am." She went on, "I will buy it for him if you don't mind?" What? Really? I already had a room full of brown stuffed horses. I did not have the storage capacity for Cozy Coupe's!

I politely explained in a shaky voice, fighting back panic and said, "It is not the money. He already has one, and he is throwing a fit because he wants another one." "I see dear. Well, it will get better one day. I promise everything will be okay, she replied." "My daughter had a young one like that and he calmed down just fine."

Let me just say, at that point, I took her words as the gospel, and her courage to approach me as divine intervention. Sometime during the interaction with that angelic woman, my son had started winding down. I scooped him up and fled Wal-Mart as quickly as possible without groceries and totally didn't care! Other than the saintly woman, I felt embarrassed, helpless, overwhelmed, and judged by the stares from others in the midst of that behavioral meltdown. Why does this have to be so hard, I remember wondering? It was not the usual toddler tantrum. Again, I was experiencing grief.

I am sure you have had your own experiences that left you feeling slighted or publicly humiliated by the stares of others. Perhaps you feel or have felt angry over the additional challenges that you and your child must face. Anger because it just isn't fair! Take a moment to work through the following questions.

Challenge Questions:

1. **Think about your own anger.**

2. **What thoughts or experiences have caused or are continuing to cause you to feel angry about your child's disability?**

3. **List all the reasons you have felt or still feel angry.**

4. **How have you dealt with that anger?**

5. **How can you let go of that anger?**

6. **Do you need to grieve the loss of "normal"? It does not mean you are grieving over the life of your child.**

7. **Who can you talk to about your anger?**

Remember: Anger is a common grief response. Talking about your anger and releasing it will help you let it go.

Chapter 8: Surfing the Waves of Guilt

Sitting in the large room, her mind drifted back to the day it all began. She remembered, they were running late as usual. Lori had developed a more personal relationship with Tommy's latest speech therapist, Dawn, and knew she would not be upset by her tardiness. In fact, they had become fairly good friends since Mike's incident. She was older than Lori but still beautiful and very kind. She had the kind of beauty that was timeless, and she looked a good ten years younger than her true age.

Tommy ran into the room and took his seat, ready to work. Routine and repetition were still his favorite companions. He was working on his expressive language skills. Lori had been practicing at home with him, she was so proud of his progress. Dawn said, "You really should go back to school and get a degree to work with children." She bragged on Lori's teaching ability with Tommy and told her it would be a waste not to share that with others. School, she thought?

Lori already had some college under her belt and always hoped she would go back later, like she had promised herself in her twenties. But the idea of going back now to focus on a specific type of professional degree seemed unlikely. Although, she had no desire to go back to an office job once Tommy was older, she thought. She is painfully aware she will have to do something full time to earn money now that she is a single parent. Time is running out. Mike's disability income for Tommy has helped keep them a float, but the ship is steadily sinking. Maybe, she thought.

Tommy was finally able to communicate basic information and loved coming to see Dawn. Lori had managed to make it through the loss of Mike and had started to make new friends, mostly those she met through Dawn. She watched Tommy categorize and practice his language skills, while laughing at the silly approaches that helped him learn. He was a beautiful, blonde-haired, green-eyed, seven-year-old who easily won the hearts of those who worked with him.

Her mind shifts back to the present as she sits in the massive, prestigious office, which is both impressive and cold. The shiver down her spine made her wish she had a jacket. The *memory of Dawn urging her to go back to school was vivid as she sat across from the president leaning back in his high-backed chair behind a huge mahogany desk. He was saying, "It's not often that my sister asks that I help someone get whatever they need to enter the university, so I tend to pay attention when she does." "You must be very special. If my sister believes in you, then so do I." He picked up the phone and called the head of financial services. He called the man by name and talked as if they were old buddies. "I'm sending someone your way and I want you to meet with her personally. I want you to make sure she gets whatever funding she needs. Consider it a personal favor."*

Lori couldn't believe what she was hearing. She shook the president's hand and thanked him. She walked downstairs to meet with the head of financial services. She could feel his questioning stare. He assessed her as she approached but quickly extended his hand. He said it was unusual to get a personal call from the president. He was obviously trying to figure out the connection, but Lori didn't take the bait. She remained quite. She felt so grateful for this new opportunity.

When Dawn told her she would talk to her brother, she had no idea that he was the president of the university. Wow! What are the odds? She is actually doing this. The reality was finally hitting her. She had no idea how she was going to manage school and Tommy as a single parent, but either way, it was happening.

The years passed, ushering in this beautiful, 70 degree day, with no clouds in sight. The air was perfect, and the campus was bustling with students all hurrying to get somewhere. The trees and flowers were in full bloom nurtured by an early spring. She was in her last semester and planned to enter graduate school in the fall. Tommy was now in the third grade and she couldn't believe how quickly time was passing. It was like she had taken a seat on the Starship Enterprise and Sulu had hit warp speed.

She couldn't believe it had already been several years since Mike left their lives and she went back to school full time. Tommy was doing pretty good overall. It had been touch and go over the past few years, but he seemed to have settled down, almost as if it was the calm before the storm. She chided herself for thinking so negatively. It was a balancing act for sure. He still had lots of therapies and school issues. He had demands that went above and beyond typical parenting that kept her mindful of the challenges that lay ahead.

She felt so guilty after Mike's incident. Poor Tommy, he had been through so much. Every day was still a struggle for him. She has just gotten used to the struggles. She has learned how to avoid tantrums, although mostly by giving in and following the yellow brick road paved by his obsessions. Pick your battles, she thinks. Deep inside, she wonders if she is creating a war that will have to be fought in the future.

Life is so hard for him. It's not fair and if she can make it up to him by making him happy, then why not! The familiar argument in her head driven by guilt and sadness is ever present and guilt always wins. So what if I give in to him. No one understands our situation. She was so deep in thought, she nearly ran into someone. "Excuse me," she said. The near miss jolted her back to school and the memory of this morning, which brought a smile to her face.

Today of all days was a day for celebration. She had been tapped by her professor this morning to be invited into Phi Kappa Phi, an honor society that recognizes both leadership skills and academic excellence. She was so honored and surprised. She felt so proud. She loved to learn and help others. It was like everything was finally falling into place. Well, almost everything, she thought.

You can do this, she chides herself. Tommy will be fine, maybe a little odd as an adult. She felt a twinge of guilt wash over her. She feels like she isn't giving Tommy enough of her time. Her mind immediately replays her shortcomings as a parent, such as giving in to his demands and letting him watch television instead of doing therapy 24/7. The unending accusations, dance in her head, making her feel guilty. Taking the easy road will place blame square on her shoulders if he doesn't reach his full potential. She feels like she is not fully devoted to him anymore because her time is divided between him, school, and life.

The first year or so after Mike's incident, she had not dated at all. It was not the time, and she was not ready. Over the past year, she had dated some, but nothing remarkable, until recently. She still feels guilty leaving Tommy for something as selfish as a date or socializing. Nonetheless, guilt or no guilt, she had started dating Robert much more frequently as of late and finds herself really liking him.

Tommy spent a lot of time with Lori's father. She was grateful that he had a grandfather to serve as a father figure in his life, since Mike was incapable of fulfilling that role. Tommy would never see his father again. He had adjusted to life without him but still talked about him from time to time. It was just her and Tommy. Just the two of them for the past several years, and they were making it just fine.

Her parents would keep Tommy one night during the week, so she could have a break. That was usually when she got together with Dawn and other friends she had made over the past few years. She convinced herself that one night away from Tommy would not wreck his world. Tonight, it would be just her and Robert again.

Robert picked her up and they headed out to eat. He had been married before and had three great kids. He was eleven years older than she and that bothered her slightly. However, he didn't look it. As much as she tried, she couldn't understand why it bothered her so much. Maybe it was just that the age difference was a big deal to society and she was afraid of standing out.

As time passed, the age difference did not matter at all anymore, at least not to her. Robert seemed to be everything she had ever wanted in a relationship. They had spent a lot of time together while Tommy was in school each day and talked about everything under the sun. Faith, family, hopes, dreams, and cooking, specifically who would do it? Somewhere along the way, Lori had begun to fall in love with Robert and knew things would only grow from here if...

Robert was handsome, smart, respectful, kind, nurturing, and confident in a humble sort of way. He loved crossword

*puzzles and the Eagles, which won him additional brownie
points. A relationship was in full bloom. The time had come for
him to meet Tommy. He knew she had a son with autism and did
not seem to be bothered by it. He never pushed to meet Tommy,
because he just wasn't a pushy person. He knew it was special,
in the next level sort of way, when Lori asked if he wanted to
meet Tommy.*

*Tommy looked handsome as usual. He had retained his
good looks as he grew. His blonde hair, green eyes, and olive
complexion were quite the combination. She pulled up to the
park and spotted Robert across the way. He caught her eyes and
started walking in their direction.*

*Remember Tommy; don't run off too far because you need
to be where mommy can see you. You are going to meet Robert,
mommy's friend. She was so nervous. She honestly did not know
what to expect. The years of living with Tommy made her very
familiar with the different looks people display. She prayed that
Robert would not have one of those looks that people get when
they are uncomfortable and don't know how to react to someone
with special needs.*

*Robert walked up to Tommy, and before he could even
speak, Tommy's small hand reached up and grabbed his, pulling
him toward the playground. He glanced down and embraced the
little hand Tommy offered him with a wide smile of kindness and
warmth. Lori's heart melted at the sight. It was as if they had
known each other for years. No awkwardness, no hesitation,
simply a boy and a man walking hand in hand. A boy too old to
be holding the man's hand would be the judgment of on lookers,
she thought.*

*Tommy's disability was not physically visible. It was the
behaviors that gave it away, if people watched long enough. But
at a glance, quick judgments could easily be made. The stares of
others were the worst sometimes. Robert proudly walked to the
playground holding his hand, completely unaware or unaffected
by the looks of others.*

*It was a touching sight to see. Her heart was full. It was
full of love, fear, and oddly guilt, but oh how she wished it could
just be full of love! Lori has felt so much guilt and fear over the*

past few years. Guilt for needing to be with adults, guilt for the time she invested in school, guilt for dating, guilt for not making everything better for Tommy, guilt for not knowing something was wrong in the pregnancy, guilt for not doing enough, guilt for trying to make Tommy do too much, guilt because he doesn't have a father, guilt, guilt, guilt! She never ignored him. She always made sure he came first, even if it meant staying up all night to study. But still she felt guilty.

Sometimes the guilt makes no sense at all and sometimes it makes perfect sense. Now she is feeling guilty for introducing him to Robert if their relationship doesn't work out leading to feelings of fear.

Tommy has such a hard time with change. He has lost so much already. The last thing he needs is to lose another man that he gets close to. What am I doing? Have you lost your mind, she screams inside her head. She tries to calm her thoughts and just be in this moment. She prays to God to protect Tommy and help her learn to trust.

Robert became a quick study of autism and of Tommy specifically. Their relationship was moving quickly, and it scared her to death. Lori decided to just lay it all out there. One night, several months later, while they were sitting on the couch, she asked Robert if he had thought about what life would be like with her and Tommy over time.

She was honest about her own fears and commitment to Tommy. She told him that she would understand if he did not want to commit to a life of caring for someone with a disability long term. She cautioned him that a commitment to her would mean a major life adjustment for him. She reminded him that there would be no travel with retirement, he would be a chronic caregiver, they would have less time as a couple, and they would never live alone without a child. She talked about the tantrums, even though Robert had seen a few by now.

Robert politely interrupted her cautions and asked, "Do you not think that I have already considered all of those things?" "I am not blind. I have thought about all the limitations and how my life will change with you and Tommy. But I would rather face a life of change and a life of possible limitations than a life without you and Tommy." The tears were stinging her eyes as she fought to keep them back. The love and sincerity in his eyes said it all. She knew in that moment that she had found a love like no other and that it belonged to her and to Tommy. Thank you God, she whispered.

Robert and Lori were married in December and began a life together by the time Tommy was nine, soon to be ten years old. She tried explaining the concept of a stepfather to Tommy, but he insisted Robert was his "new dad" and Mike was the "old dad". The titles he chose stuck, and from that day forward, that is how he referred to them. Lori was in graduate school working on her master's degree. Robert fully supported her.

There were many days in the beginning that were full of laughter, love, and challenges. Lori thinks about the meltdown this morning and yesterday and last week. They seem to be getting worse. Robert just doesn't know Tommy well enough yet to avoid all the meltdowns. Even though he had spent a lot of time with him, it is different when you live with him and start messing with his daily routines.

This morning Robert took a different way to school and Tommy cried for hours, even after being dropped off at school. Tommy has no toleration for change. His need for repetition is like the need for oxygen when you've been underwater for a long time. She also wasn't prepared for all the challenges that have occurred with merging two families. She reflects back on the first time she met James, Robert's youngest son, her now stepson. He was only two years younger than Tommy, but he might as well have been twenty years older.

He has regular visitation with his dad, which now means visitation with her and Tommy too. The up close and personal contrast that James forced her to face in her own home was, without a doubt, the most emotionally troubling adjustment she was completely unprepared for.

Tommy was an only child. At home he could be himself. They had their own routines and rituals that were normal for them. At least it had become their norm, and without a comparison, it felt natural, not weird. James changed everything. It wasn't his fault that he was a typical boy. He did not warm up to Tommy from the start and things still haven't changed. He wasn't mean to him, just dismissive and standoffish.

James was just a kid, but still, she could feel some resentment building. She felt sorry for Tommy and it was almost like she resented James for being "normal" and shining a spotlight on Tommy's limitations and weirdness. His rejection of Tommy caused pain at home, her once sanctuary from pain. She had to face these feelings at school functions and church but never in her own home.

What am I going to do? She felt guilty for feeling resentment and jealousy towards a child. She hid her feelings from James, but she still lived with them inside her own head. Great, now I have something else to feel guilty about, she thought. She knew it wasn't right, but how was she supposed to stop her feelings? It will get better, she thought. Just give it time.

Robert's other two children were much older. Carrie, his daughter, was in college and Scott, his oldest son, was eighteen years old. Carrie was pretty and smart with a dazzling personality. Scott was handsome like Robert and basically, a good young man. Both were accepting of Tommy, however, whether visits were sweet or awkward, they did not live in the same house. When the visits ended, Tommy and Lori had the sanctuary they were used to in the privacy of their own home.

James was a different story. To make matters worse, James' mother did not want her son to spend time around Robert and Lori, mostly because she was jealous and fearful that Robert would try to get custody of James. At least, this is what Lori thought. Lori did not understand her fears. They were unfounded. Robert had no intentions of attempting to get custody of James.

Months passed, and there was a request to meet with the attorney who had handled Robert and his ex-wife's divorce years ago. As they sat in the attorney's office, the man began to hand Robert and Lori papers. Lori could not believe it! You are kidding me, she blurted out. She felt rage deep inside and disbelief that people could be so cruel. James's mother had filed a motion to stop James from visitation on the grounds that he was *too fearful of Tommy and it was, in turn, causing him physical symptoms. She also charged that Robert did not give James enough autonomy.*

They had taken James to a child counselor who was working towards gaining her professional license in her perspective field. This counselor in training had never met Robert, Lori, or Tommy. The counselor had inaccurately placed a diagnosis on Tommy based on the information provided by Robert's ex-wife. The "professional" in training documented incidents that never occurred between Tommy and James, yet they were written as factual. This counselor released the information to the courts as record in an attempt to deny visitation.

"Is this legal?" Lori asked. "How can this professional, who has never met my son or me, place a diagnosis on him?" She was dumbfounded. Angry to the core that anyone would try to use Tommy's disability as a weapon, she could feel the blood turning her cheeks red.

The attorney began saying, "I understand your anger Lori, and truth be told, I would be angry if someone said those things about my son." "It's obvious this is a ploy to try to deny visitation." Super, she thought. As if life was not complicated before, now there was a battle with the ex-wife over visitation, hinging on Tommy. I'm not up for this, she thought. She felt the need to protect Robert and Tommy both.

She checked her own emotion at the door and agreed to fight: Fight for her husband, fight for Tommy, and fight for James. Robert was a good father and this was all so unfair. She felt responsible somehow, as if this was punishment for Robert because he opened his heart and life to her and Tommy. If Tommy did not have autism, this would not even be an issue. The thought made her even angrier.

Again, she felt guilty that somehow she had caused this because she was in Roberts's life. Poor Tommy, she thought. What kind of a person uses a child's disability to manipulate the system for selfish motive? It was beyond her comprehension.

The age difference between James, Carrie, and Scott, his older sister and brother, created more of an only child experience for James. In time, Lori began to realize that James had been coddled to the extent that he did not know how to swing on a playground, ride a bike, and fear ruled his thoughts. It wasn't that he lacked capability, but his grandmother, who was his primary caregiver while his mother worked, kept him in a bubble.

She was creating an environment where everything revolved around James, and his comfort was first and foremost. The belief systems etched into James's life were: If the world is unsafe or if you don't want it or like it, then you don't have to do it. Robert would try to throw a baseball to him or teach him to ride a bike and he would cry. Lori really started to feel sorry for James in much the same way as Tommy.

He is being shaped by his environment in unhealthy ways. The irony is thick. The very people telling the "professional" how fearful James is of Tommy and how he doesn't like being around him, are also the bubble makers that are creating fear. It is baffling. The truth is James needs someone to help him learn how to conquer his fears. He needs someone to show him that he will be okay, so that he will learn to do all that he is capable of doing. The whole ordeal wrapped up with a nasty trial.

The court house was cold and Lori was shaking. She is shaking partly from the cold, but mostly from nervous energy surrounding the day. Today is the day of testimony and the court's decision on visitation. It will all soon be over. It had been a year since the day in the attorney's office, and a tough year at that. James has been coming for visitation and is doing fine. The whole thing seems like a huge waste of time and resources. James shows no fear of Tommy whatsoever.

The "professional" counselor in training had been sanctioned by her governing board for unethical practices. She was reprimanded for diagnosing a child she had never met and releasing her findings to a third party. Her information was based on hearsay rather than facts. She was also investigated by the state's district attorney's office, prompted by her own board, to evaluate for possible legal violations. Lori, at least feels like Tommy has received some justice in the actions taken against this "so- called" professional.

The decision was rendered by the judge that James should continue visitation and was not in any danger or harm. In fact, the judge stressed the importance of the father/son relationship and urged the two parents to find a way to work together. Tommy never knew about any of it, but James knew way too much. His mind had been saturated with discriminatory beliefs about Tommy and his own father. She and Robert never spoke of it in front of the children, so Lori knew where James was getting his information. Why? Because selfish people care more about their own interest than what is best for the children, she thought.

To use one child's disability as grounds to deny another child a relationship with his father is below the belt and reveals a lack of basic humanity, Lori thought. She knew the road to forgiveness would be long and hard. She also knew the continued interactions with Robert's ex would be strained for years to come. How do you have a good relationship with someone who attempted to use your child's disability for selfish gain and retaliation against the man you love? She knew the answer; there would be no good relationship. She could only hope for forgiveness one day in the future.

The holidays came and went as the seasons changed with the passing of time. The blending of the two families was an emotional bowl of alphabet soup. Sad, lonely, isolated, uncomfortable, regretful, and guilty, all well hidden under a smile and wishes for a Merry Christmas or happy Fourth of July, depending on the holiday. Of course there was joy, but the joy would inevitably get choked out by the unexpected emotional pain with each new challenge. The challenges were many.

The guilt was the worst. She felt responsible in some way as Tommy retreated into his own world, unable to connect to this new family. She remembered years past, when she was able to give all of her time and attention to him, but now, he disappears into the background as others compete for attention in ways he cannot compete.

She needed some way to ease her guilt and give Tommy joy, regardless of what anyone else thinks. Why not indulge him? And that is what she did. She bought him whatever he wanted and catered to his every whim, as much as possible. Deep inside, she knew over-indulgence was not sound parenting, but it made her feel better to see him happy. She felt sorry for him that life had to be so hard. People dismissed him. She dismissed him at times. She felt like their lives were best described as trying to make a square peg fit into a round hole.

She realized she was beginning to resent people who had "normal" lives, easy lives. She resented so much these days. The guilt of the hardship her son bore was becoming more of a driving force in her thoughts than she wanted, but she felt helpless to change it. He is moving towards his teen years and the thought of that fact sent panic throughout her body. She is running out of time. Tommy is running out of time.

Lori seems to be struggling with guilt if she is not completely focused on Tommy at all times. It is easy to see the huge sense of responsibility she feels for his happiness. She also appears to be blaming herself if he fails or faces difficult circumstances. You may be reading Lori's story and wondering why she feels so guilty. Or you may identify with her guilt. The guilt we experience as part of the Atypical Cyclic grief process can be far reaching and can be connected to many different thoughts and events.

Remember Nicole from Chapter 6? Remember the doctor who told her that it was her sin that caused her son to have autism. The guilt she experienced was caused by someone else who told her untruths. But what do we tell ourselves? Do we blame ourselves at times if not enough progress is being made? Do we feel guilty because we feel the loss is made worse by something we are doing or not doing? Do we feel guilty when we feel sad because our child has a disability that causes hardships?

Do we chide ourselves when we grieve because a good parent should never have those feelings? I certainly did. You may not feel like you have the right to feel grief or loss because, at least you have your child, and there are many positive aspects to their life and even disability. It may feel like you are simply focusing on the negative and not valuing your child as a "good parent" should.

No one likes to feel guilty. To avoid the feelings of guilt, you may put all of your emotional energy into "making them better," or "making them happy," just like Lori does. Pushing down the feelings of guilt instead of letting them out and working through them contributes to poor adapting. Remember, it is the loss of "normal" and the challenges that causes our grief, not our children. It is okay to grieve. We don't have to fix everything. We cannot fix everything!

Guilt can affect how we parent, as we can witness with Lori here. In my research, I found an article about counseling children with hearing loss and special needs written by David Luterman in 2004. I found it very interesting and it definitely struck a nerve. He suggests that, "Guilt is usually felt by parents of children with special needs. The mother's guilt is often related to 'cause' and the father's guilt is often related to his 'failure to protect the family'."

He goes on to explain that guilt that results from a sense of responsibility or cause in parents of a child diagnosed with a disability can create unhealthy parenting behaviors. These unhealthy parenting behaviors may negatively impact the child or the family.

Parents who feel a sense of self-blame or huge weight of responsibility may internalize guilt. This silent guilt could result in either becoming overprotective or over-dedicated. He explains that an overprotective parent can cause a child to become fearful with a limited ability to cope with the world independently. An over dedicated parent can lead to dysfunctional families because not enough energy is given to maintain the entire family.

If you have several children and one of them has a disability, the additional challenges presented by the disability can demand more attention, which can result in too little attention for the other children in the family without disabilities. I only had one child, but the time and energy I invested in his development to "catch up" left little to no room for anyone else in my life. I was definitely the over dedicated parent fueled by irrational guilt that I somehow caused his autism or didn't do enough to fix it. In those early years, I literally spent all of my time energy and thoughts focused on my son's progress. I was chasing "normal" with everything I had.

Guilt is a powerful emotion. My over dedication had negative impacts on my marriage and personal relationships with friends. I placed nothing or no one above my son, except maybe God, and sometimes I am not even sure about that in those early years. I was way out of balance and didn't even know it. There is nothing wrong with doing all that you can to help your child progress and reach his/her full potential. We SHOULD do that! I am talking about extreme behaviors.

The sense of over responsibility caused by guilt produces a strong need to keep them safe! We want to keep them safe from harm, teasing, judgment, criticism, and rejection. That is an impossible task and unrealistic expectation for any parent.

The guilt in ACG can cause us to overcompensate for the loss. Let's be honest here. If you watch your child struggle in so many areas, it is natural to want to comfort them and make them happy. After all, every parent wants their child to be happy and loved. Guilt can cause parents to over compensate, which can interfere with our ability to parent effectively. Lori has really started to overcompensate, because she feels so guilty for somehow letting Tommy down.

This is not unique to A-typical Cyclic Grief. Think about parents who have recently divorced. It is not uncommon for parents to feel guilty that the family has split apart. They see their children as struggling, and so they will overlook things and be much more lenient than in the past. They might even indulge them more with gifts or treats. They are trying to compensate for their child's loss. Guilt can cloud our judgment.

Overcompensating or being overprotective can be particularly impactful for our children because many of them do not push for independence in traditional ways or at the expected naturally occurring progression. Think about it. Overprotective parents of typical kids usually get pushback from their child if they are being overprotective. Typical kids push for independence. Unfortunately, that is not always the case with children with special needs. Yes, they will push for independence at times, but they often like routine and need assistance more than typical children. Sometimes, this can create stagnant patterns for parents, or maybe even ruts, if we are not careful.

Our sense of responsibility that causes feelings of guilt can keep us stuck in patterns of over protection and over dedication. It may happen more often than we realize. I remember when I remarried. My son's stepfather, who I refer to as his father, is wonderful at bringing patterns of overprotection to my attention that I honestly do not even see.

For example, a few years after we were married, he had been solely responsible for taking our son to the barber shop. You know, it was a guy thing. One day he was not able, so I took our son. I was sharing the experience with my husband and he asked, "Why did you go in with him?" I immediately panicked and thought, "Oh my goodness, he has been sending him in alone." After much discussion, my husband helped me realize he was perfectly capable of going in alone, and in fact, felt proud that he was on his own. From that day forward, he went in alone. I would have never sent him in alone but only because I was still operating from past experiences, patterns, and a full awareness of all the possibilities of what could go wrong. Fear, dedication, and protective instincts ruled my patterns. My husband was seeing potential, not limitations.

Challenge yourself to look at your own behaviors. Are you stuck in some patterns you need to change? Are there things your child could be doing on his/her own, even if it is slightly scary?

My hope is you will start recognizing and challenging feelings of guilt! You will recognize stagnant patterns, over-dedication, and overcompensating, all fueled by guilt. The vast majority of parents would never intentionally bring harm to their children! I did not harm my child. My child was and still is impaired by a developmental disability, but I was not the cause. You are not the cause.

Guilt was definitely at work in my life when my son was young. I had no idea how much A-typical Cyclic Grief was impacting my life, my marriage, and my emotions. Again, I did not see this over dedication or overprotective reaction to guilt as a response to grief. I also did not see the path of dysfunction I was sprinting down at a remarkably fast pace. Pause here to reflect on the following questions.

Challenge Questions:

1. Have you experienced feelings of guilt?

2. If so, what makes you feel guilty?

3. Is your guilt because you somehow feel responsible or feel like you didn't protect your child?

4. Are you over dedicated or over protective? Or both?

5. Are your behaviors interfering with your child's growth towards independence?

6. What changes can you make to regain some balance? Do you need to spend more time with your other children, spouse, or friends?

Remember: This journey is a marathon NOT a sprint!

Chapter 9: Marriage Dangers: Detour Ahead.

It was the perfect night. She couldn't remember the last time they had been out alone, just the two of them. They had dinner and even danced. Robert looked as handsome as ever but the continued stress at home and work was taking a toll. She was wondering when things started to turn. Robert and Lori, it was the perfect union, at least in her mind.

They shared long, eye- to-eye gazes that revealed the depths of their soul and where time stood still. She still has the CD Robert made for her when their love was growing. It was a collection of love songs he made for her to express his love and the tenderness of their relationship. All her friends were so jealous.

Robert was romantic, smart, accomplished and good looking, the total package. Her mind drifted back to the present, as he continued talking about work. These days the topic of conversation was either work or Tommy. Things were hard. Tommy was not doing well behaviorally. The teen years were starting off with a bang.

Tensions were high at school, and Lori was in a state of high alert all the time. Robert had commented several times in the past that it felt like their lives were consumed with Tommy. He told her he understood how hard it was, but if they did not make time for themselves as a couple, he feared they would not be able to withstand the journey. He never threatened divorce but hoped for more time together and more of a balance.

Lori's mind drifts to the most recent fight they had over Tommy. Robert was angry because he felt like all she cared about was Tommy. She was angry because Robert was demanding more than she could give; at least that is how she felt. In fact, she felt like she had nothing to give, and that is probably the biggest problem. She is giving nothing to Robert. They haven't had sex in over a month and forget spending time together. Those were topics of complaint during their last argument and the ones before that too.

The stress was killing her. She was so tired by the end of each day and consumed with worry that she had nothing left. Robert just doesn't get it. He doesn't see it the same as she does.

He doesn't have to walk the halls of that school and feel the stares and negativity aimed at Tommy. Robert wanted Tommy to play sports a few years ago and even coached his soccer team. That was a disaster. Robert eventually gave up the idea that he could teach Tommy how to play sports. The reality started to sink in. He started assuming a more supportive but less hands on role with Tommy.

He went to work every day to his "normal" job with "normal" people. He has his "normal" kids, who play sports, and did all the things that father's hope they would do. Lori wondered if his ability to accept Tommy so easily was partly due to his other children. He got to experience raising typical kids and did not have to worry if they would ever live independently. Lori felt the resentment rising up inside her. He just doesn't understand how it feels to be his mother.

Robert was talking as Lori drifted back to the conversation at hand. He was assuring her that everything would be okay with Tommy. He was talking about his own needs, and she lost it. She raised her voice and told Robert that "he had no idea if things would be okay with Tommy, and it was easy for him to say they would be because he already had three other children!" She saw the hurt in his eyes and regretted her words immediately.

Balance, she thought, what is that? How do you have balance when you don't even know if your son will be able to stay in school? You wonder if you will be able to hold down a job or will have to stay at home to care for him the rest of your life. Will you be able to have a life with some normalcy in it? She felt another twinge of resentment towards Robert, even though she knew he was right. She wondered if balance was easier for people when they were not in jeopardy of losing anything. He will still go to work if Tommy can't go to school. He will still have adult socialization. He will still have some normalcy. She felt terrible for her thoughts but felt powerless to stop them.

She loved Robert and Tommy both so much it hurt. She felt pulled. Life would have been simpler if she would have just stayed single, she thought. Then, she would not have had to share her time or love. She would not feel pulled or resentful.

The thought of life without Robert made her want to cry on the spot. No way! I would rather be pulled completely apart than imagine my life without him, she decided. He is Tommy's dad now, and he loves him very much.

Here we go again, she thought. I am in the emotional washing machine and it just reached the spin cycle, she smirks at the analogy of her thoughts and emotions. Back and forth, twisting and turning, maybe I should have stayed single, no I should have married, maybe I should've and maybe I shouldn't have, always second guessing her decisions, especially when it comes to Tommy. Will she ever get out of this spin cycle? she wonders.

She gently reached over and held Robert's hand. She apologized for what she said earlier. He returned a warm smile. Their marriage was strained not because they were unkind to one another or fell out of love. But because the outside stress of work and autism was stripping them of precious time and focus they needed to keep the relationship healthy. When they fell in love, they were spending a lot of time together and the relationship was important.

She felt like a failure. Can't I do anything right? she wondered. I can't stop fighting for Tommy but I can't stop fighting for my marriage either. Lori honestly did not know how to find balance. She looked at his face and saw the strain he was trying to conceal behind his smile. She wondered if he regretted the decision to marry her. She would understand. After all, how could he have possibly known what to expect. She didn't even expect this! Somehow they have to make it together.

Lori starts to cry and tells Robert her thoughts and fears. He gently hugs her, and they talk about changes they can make that would give them some time together but not at the complete sacrifice of Tommy. Robert tells her how much he cares about Tommy too, but he also believes if they are not in a good place, then they will not be able to help Tommy. He reminds her that they have to be able to care for him over his lifetime, not just the teen years. "We are running a marathon not a sprint," he says. "If we run out of steam or break apart, we will not be able to keep going to complete our race."

Lori thinks about the comparison to a marathon and how runners have to be in good physical condition. They have to make time to train and eat healthy to be able to withstand the long distance run. She decides to work on taking care of herself better and invest time in her marriage so it can go the distance. She hugs Robert and enjoys the rest of their evening together, promising to have more nights like this soon. She sees a slight spark in his eyes that had not been there earlier and it makes her feel really hopeful for a brighter future...

Marriage can be challenging with or without kids. When unusual circumstances are piled on top of the relationship, it can go from challenging to downright overwhelming. Marriages tend to become very strained when all or most of our time, finances, and emotions are consumed by a single event or situation. Having a child with a disability can create such a situation.

As a counselor in private practice, I provide marriage counseling as part of my services. The demands of parenting, work, and life wreak havoc on relationships unless couples learn to be intentional and invest time in their marriage. Let's talk about what I call "Maintaining the Baseline."

I describe relationship development as happening in phases. We will talk about the New Phase, the Baseline Phase, and the Declining Phase. After we talk about the phases, we will talk about how to protect our relationships. We will also explore how the impacts of ACG add additional danger zones for couples raising a child or children with disability.

The New Phase of the relationship describes the start. You know the old cliché "the sparks are flying." This is the phase where people typically invest high levels of time in the relationship. They will show intense interest. It's the "getting to know you" phase. At this point, people are placing high priority on the relationship. You smell good and pay special attention to making yourself as attractive as possible.

You turn down outings with friends to spend time with your new heartthrob. It is exciting times with exploding emotions that release feel good endorphins. Adrenaline is pumping with lots of romantic gestures in the mix. Intimacy is forming and couples may spend lots of time together talking and connecting. High levels of energy are expended on the relationship. This phase is not sustainable over time because life goes on and other things eventually need our time and attention as well. The newness starts to wear off, and the relationship moves into the Baseline Phase.

During the Baseline phase, people invest more moderate levels of time. The relationship is still thriving and very important but people begin to start sharing their time with others again. The couple is still curious and learning about one another. They are learning patterns and habits. They are getting more comfortable sharing life in everyday scenarios. The pressure is not there to look their best at every encounter. But appearance is still maintained and romance is still alive. Intimacy is maturing but still going strong. The butterflies or jitters are not as noticeable. The excitement is diminishing but still there and the relationship is fulfilling. It is normalizing in this phase. Remember the first phase is not sustainable, because it has to normalize at some point.

The Baseline Phase is important because this is when the expectations or ideals of the long term functioning of the relationship are formed. In other words, the relationship is defined during this phase.

The levels of intimacy, communication, time, romance, and respect are all defined. If your partner is spontaneous and romantic, then you expect they will always be romantic and spontaneous. If you have high levels of intimacy, you will expect continued high levels of intimacy in the future. Energy levels normalize and a baseline develops. This baseline is usually what people will refer back to when things start to decline. We have all either said or heard some of these references before such as: "We aren't as close as we used to be" and "We don't talk like we use to." We tend to believe that things will remain consistent over time.

In healthy relationships, things can remain intimate and close over time; however, it takes continued investment. Things will never stay exactly the same and that would be an unrealistic expectation. However, people can grow together and have their love grow with them in healthy ways.

The Declining Phase is where dissatisfaction starts to creep in because things do not continue as we thought they would. Many things in life contribute to the decrease in time given to our partners. This phase describes the pitfalls relationships experience when investment stops or is not enough to maintain some level of consistency.

The Declining Phase usually does not happen overnight. It is much more subtle and often difficult to recognize. After the vows, most people know each other pretty well at that point. There are always exceptions; but overall, most people do not have arranged marriages in today's society. They feel certain they know who they are marrying and have chosen that person of their own free will.

In the Declining Phase, the "I want to get to know you" behavior is often replaced with "I already know you" behavior. This shift in thinking moves communication away from intimacy and is replaced with the more superficial day to day conversations such as "How was your day at work?" etc. Conversation revolves around the children, work, friends, and schedules but rarely around intimate feelings for each other or the relationship.

Communication and connectedness begin to decline. As life continues to throw demands our way, the relationship tends to get what's left over. Time investment in the relationship tends to take a backseat to work obligations, taking care of children, and social obligations. Relationships move from first on the list of priorities, to not even making it into the top 10. Intimacy can turn into something that is scheduled or a source of conflict between the couple. Romantic gestures often disappear. Keeping ourselves attractive for our lover is no longer a priority. In fact, it can become unimportant all together in some cases. After all, once you wake up together day after day what does it matter? This becomes the mindset.

I have worked with couples who have been married for twenty plus years, and once the children leave for college; they land in counseling trying to save their marriage from divorce.

The common complaint I hear is they feel like they are strangers. They wake up one day and realize they no longer know or possibly love the person sharing their bed, at least not in a romantic way. They want to be connected again. They want love and romance and if not with each other, with someone.

Would any of us expect to remain close friends with someone we never had more than a superficial conversation with for the past 20 plus years? Sure, we might still love them or at least the memory of our time when we were close friends, but it is more of a memory than an on-going relationship. Most of us would not expect to maintain a close friendship with no investment. Why would we expect that from our marriages?

The Declining Phase marks the start of the danger zone for all couples. Co-existing and co-parenting do not equal a relationship. Roommates can get along perfectly but it does not make them intimate or romantic.

The Declining Phase is especially dangerous for parents raising a child or children with a disability. The additional challenges or necessary treatments for the child with a disability usually take more time, money, and emotional energy than the care for typical children. The additional financial cost may cause people to have to work more and, therefore, have less time for the marriage. It can cause more marital strife and arguments surrounding money or lack of money.

Sometimes people have to travel for treatment or therapies causing separation from a spouse or partner. Sometimes one parent or both have to fight school systems to get services for their children, which can result in legal battles. Not to mention the impact of A-typical Cyclic Grief, which can create overprotection or over-dedication, throwing marriages out of balance.

Gender differences in how we process grief and approach parenting can create tension in marriages. Fathers oftentimes feel a sense of failure for not being able to protect their child and their wife from the difficulties. It is not uncommon for men to feel the loss of the son they dreamed they would have that may play sports etc. Men connect differently than women do. Men tend to bond over activities such as golf, football, and sports in general.

In contrast, women tend to bond through conversation and sharing of intimate conversation.

Society affects how men and women grieve differently. You have heard the saying, "Big boys don't cry." Boys are taught to suck it up and act like a man. Basically, they are told to just tuck all their emotions inside and just deal with it. It is far more acceptable for women to show emotion in our society than men. Think about how that impacts pillow talk and general conversations between mom and dad about their child who is experiencing losses.

The additional demands that are experienced both emotionally and physically because of a disability cause the declining phase to be more complicated in marriages. The good news is, "Where there is a will, there is a way." We can find time for our significant other. It is important that you create a team approach to parenting. Learn to talk about the feelings of loss, denial dangers, anger, guilt, and other emotions associated with A-typical Cyclic Grief. If money is tight, have a picnic in your living room after the kids are asleep. Find creative ways to carve out your time together. So how do we protect our relationships from becoming another statistic? Here are some helpful strategies.

1. We have to move OUT of the danger zone. Take your relationship temperature. Step back and look at your time and how you spend it together. It is a fact that people change over time. The man or woman that you married years ago has changed. Are you the same person you were 5 or 10 years ago? Of course not! You have matured. Your dreams or expectations may have changed. Think about how you have changed over the past years. Does your partner know your thoughts, fears, ambitions, dreams, sorrows, and joys? Ask your partner how they have changed? Are they happy with the relationship? Are they lonely? Scared? Overwhelmed? Comfort each other. Form an alliance. Become re-acquainted with your partner. Turn the TV, cell phones, and other technology off, face each other, and start asking these questions.

2. Readjust your priorities. If you have set a date with your partner then honor it. In the same way you would keep a doctor's appointment, a work meeting, etc, you should give your marriage the same respect. It takes commitment to make your relationship a priority. If you do not have access to childcare, then figure out a time, even if it is a few minutes before you go to sleep, to connect, share your feelings, and be open. You may have to seek out a child or adult sitter service and pay to get a night out. Maybe once a month, go out as a couple. *Remember you were a couple at the start of this journey and if you want to be a couple at the end, you have to act like a couple in the middle.* On a side note, a couple means 2, not 3 or 4, just you and your partner. I know you love your children, but if your children are with you all the time, that is not couple time, that is family time. If you are with another couple that is not couple time, it is time with friends. There is a big difference. Sometimes you need time alone just like you had during the Baseline phase!

3. Add romantic gestures back into your lives. Leave a note, bring a cup of coffee, and be flirtatious if the mood strikes. If you start connecting again in meaningful ways, the feelings of romance will most likely return. However, it would be very easy to dismiss the need to do something romantic. Just do it. Think about how you would feel if your partner surprised you with a romantic act. Remember how you used to look your best before that special date. Take time to invest in putting your best foot forward for your partner. We all want and need to feel loved and appreciated.

4. Plan some fun activities together. Do something enjoyable both with and without the kids at times. Play together! Think about when the baseline was being established. You most likely had times you played together. Whether that was hanging out or a physical activity, you had some good times together. Those

memories are just that. Create more memories and continue to create memories. The past does not sustain the future indefinitely.

5. Finally, treat your partner as well as you would an acquaintance. Let's be honest. We all tend to smile and show our best side to those we encounter throughout our day at work or in the community. When we were establishing our baseline, we were still giving our partner our best. If we had a bad day, we might talk about it with them rather than take it out on them. If we were tired from a long day at work or in life, we were still happy to see them. We did not come home and drown ourselves in technology or anything else to escape the pressures of life, leaving them to fend for themselves. If we had, chances are, we would have never ended up married or committed for life. Sometimes we show acquaintances more respect and kindness than we do the people we claim to hold dearest.

Beware of the danger zone lures. The distractions we face are like lures tempting us to invest time in everything other than our relationship. These lures hypnotize us into believing nothing else is more important than them and the relationship can wait. We will make all kind of excuses and justifications. We can't spend time this weekend because the kids have a track meet. We can't the week after that because it is mom's birthday. The list goes on and on and on. Ask yourself this question:

If my marriage relationship was a living person, am I giving that person what they need to survive? Would that person be starving to death? Are you feeding him or her every day? A relationship is alive and needs to be fed daily to survive!

You have to make the relationship a priority with equal importance. Again, BALANCE is KEY! Take time to work through the following questions. Challenge your partner to read this chapter and talk about these questions together. Work on a plan to get back to that baseline!

Challenge Questions:

1. What is your relationship temperature?

2. Do you have symptoms of decline?

3. How can you readjust your priorities to make your relationship equally as important as your children and career?

4. When can you plan some time with your partner to talk and reconnect? Think of some questions you would like to ask them.

5. Are you willing to talk openly about your feelings? If you are experiencing A-typical Cyclic Grief, share those feelings with your partner.

6. What romantic or spontaneous acts can you do to show your partner you love them?

Remember: You were a couple at the start of this journey and if you want to be a couple at the end, you have to act like a couple in the middle.

Chapter 10: The Battlefield in my Homeland

Lori's heart sank as the phone rang. Every day she was on pins and needles hoping Tommy would make it through the day without getting a call from the school. She answered the phone, "Hello..." "I understand. Yes, I'm on my way." She grabbed her purse and headed for the door. Today was not going to be one of the days he made it. The middle school principal asked her to pick him up from school because he was acting out and had hit one of his teachers. It was a regular occurrence these days. If he was not hitting a teacher, then it would just be something else.

She arrived at school to see Tommy sitting in the office with a look on his face she had seen many times before. The middle school principal pulled her into his office for a "word." "Mrs. Jones," he said, "I'm just not sure how much more of this we can tolerate." "I'm so sorry," she said. "We are working very hard at home to help him learn how to communicate his feelings, instead of acting out physically."

The principal said, "You know, Mrs. Jones, it seems to me you work really hard to try and make everything better for Tommy. His life isn't going to always be perfect. Don't you think that other parents want everything to be just right for their kids too? My son is graduating this year from high school, and don't you think I had dreams of him attending Harvard? Well, he isn't going to Harvard. He is just going to a local college. Don't you think that tears me up? Well, it does."

He continued saying, "Take my advice, Mrs. Jones. You need to just let Tommy start figuring things out on his own instead of trying to fix everything for him. I am going to be honest with you. Most of the teachers don't want to work with Tommy, mainly because of you. They don't want to have to deal with you." "Just take him home and bring him back tomorrow," said the middle school principal, and "think about what I said."

Lori was speechless! She could not believe that man had just compared her son's autism to his son having to go to a local college instead of Harvard. The tears welled up in her eyes; his harsh words stinging her deep down inside. Tommy can't even survive on his own, so how is he supposed to figure all this out.

He doesn't have the ability to figure it all out. The tears ran down her cheeks as she walked away from the principal headed towards Tommy. She felt so much shame. If Tommy could just graduate from high school with a regular diploma, but the thought caused a deep wave of pain.

Tommy is currently reading at a fourth grade level and most all of his academic work falls somewhere in the elementary school range. He is fourteen years old and moving towards high school, working on a certificate of attendance. She would give anything if Tommy was able to be typical like the middle school principal's son, and graduate high school headed for "the local college". If she had the privilege of letting him figure things out on his own, it would be a miracle from God. She has fought so hard for Tommy to receive the services that he desperately needs at school. Isn't that what a mother is supposed to do, she wondered?

The teachers don't want to work with my son and it's my fault. She weeps silently in her mind, as tears roll quietly down her face. How could he say those things, she wondered? The thought of sending Tommy back to that school tomorrow made her sick. She is overcome by sorrow, shame, anger, and fear.

She walked with Tommy to the car. He was talking loudly to everyone and no one at the same time. It's what they call echolalia. It is sort of like a parrot effect; however, his is delayed and not connected to anything immediately spoken. He was very upset, and she knew it would be a few hours before they were able to work through the emotional waves that were yet to come.

She reflected back on the hours of school meetings dedicated to help Tommy with his behavior and education. The legal expenses to hire an attorney to ensure the school would comply with the law to provide him what he needed and the hours spent learning about the law. The emotional and financial drain is still taking its toll on her today. It is still taking its toll on her marriage.

Unfortunately, none of the schools have been able to follow the Individualized Education Program that tells them how to deal with Tommy's challenging behavior. They agree to the program but don't follow it, which always seems to lead to a negative outcome. She brings this up at meetings, and with teachers, as well as staff, but they all get defensive, and make her feel like she is being unreasonable.

Why doesn't anything seem to be the right combination to unlock Tommy's potential or simply give us a peaceful existence, she thought? It feels like an emotional battle every day she has to face the stares when she walks down the halls of his school, the chastising tone of the middle school principal, the well-meaning advice of others, the judgment, others avoiding her, and worst of all, her helplessness to change it.

She feels like an alien from Mars trying to fit into life on planet earth. She was pretty sure that most people thought of her as an alien with an alien child wreaking havoc on their young earthlings.

She was well read on the subject of autism. Since the diagnosis, her focus and mission in life has been to learn everything about autism and how to be the best advocate and rehabilitator for her son. She wanted him to have access to all of the treatments available to overcome this obstacle. She started him in therapy before he was ever diagnosed with autism. He was behind other kids his age but she always believed in a brighter future. If she just pushed harder and never gave up on the idea that he could live a "normal" life, then he would.

She was not going to let a diagnosis stop her from seeing Tommy succeed. She remembered all the birthday parties and play-dates when he was younger. All her attempts to make sure his life experiences were just like all the other kids. Apparently, she should be ashamed of herself for trying to make his life better, according to the principal, she thinks bitterly. If he only knew, she whispers.

She remembers the years of Applied Behavioral Analysis therapy (ABA) and every other alphabet soup type of therapy you could think of that was supposed to help Tommy catch up. All the tantrums and long hours of interventions that he called play, those were the tough years.

She thought by the time he was a teenager things would be settling down and life would be more normal. They had seen so many glimpses of "normal" throughout the years, but it always seemed to be just out of reach. She was not prepared for this new battlefield. It was not easier! In fact, it was the hardest yet. Her focus used to be on academic and social gains. Now, it is on daily survival. Not just surviving Tommy's behavior but surviving the emotional waves of guilt, anger, shame, defeat, isolation, and anxiety that occur every time she interacts with people. No one understands! Worse yet, she doesn't even know who she could tell without sounding like a terrible mother. She sent Tommy down to his room once they arrived home.

Now she hears him yelling in his room at the top of his lungs but she does not go check on him. She has realized he needs space to let out some emotion first before trying to talk about what has happened. Then, she heard a loud crash. She ran downstairs to make sure he was okay and she was dumbfounded by what she saw. Tommy had ripped some of the pictures off his wall and thrown them on the floor with such force that they were broken all around him.

What has happened to my son, she wondered? His outbursts have become aggressive and unpredictable. Scary! Sad! She was shell- shocked by this new behavior. Tears welled up in her eyes. She immediately called Robert to come home from work to help her calm Tommy and deal with this meltdown.

Robert came home as soon as he could break away. By the time he got home, Tommy had begun to calm down. He was now crying uncontrollably and Lori was holding him. Robert came over and patted Tommy on the back telling him everything would be okay. He then started to clean up the mess, while Lori continued to console their son.

What are we going to do, she asked Robert? "I don't know," he answered. "We will get through this," he reassures her. "Tommy is going through a tough time right now and we have to hang in there with him. Things will get better," Robert said. I hope so, she thought. I hope so.

Lori was having lunch with her coworkers later that week, listening to their conversations, not sure what to say or how to join in. Sally was bragging about her son playing football and the new girlfriend. June was going on about her son's ACT

99

scores and college applications.

What is she supposed to say? Tommy didn't get sent home from school yesterday, however, he destroyed his room earlier in the week. She has learned to just say Tommy is good when someone asks. She would say things like, he is shy and really just likes to play video games. She doesn't dare tell them the truth. It was like she is protecting Tommy in some strange way by keeping his challenges to herself. She also knew her hopes for Tommy were miles apart from the conversations of her coworkers.

If only her life could be that simple. If only her worries were which college Tommy would attend or whether or not she liked the new girlfriend. She felt the urge to scream or cry but knows she has to remain silent. She has learned through the years that people become uncomfortable when she talks about Tommy and his autism. They just don't know what to say, so the default response is to spin it as rainbow- colored. They will ask if he is a genius and talk about what they know based on Hollywood's portrayal of autism in the movie Rain Man.

She wouldn't know how to express all the emotions floating inside her mind, even if she thought people were comfortable with the topic. She feels cheated, frustrated, scared, worried, responsible, helpless, out of control, and totally devoted to Tommy. This is not what she expected when she became a mom. She should be talking about sports, girlfriends, and academic achievements, not worried about whether or not he will make it through the day without a meltdown.

She snaps back to the conversation at hand to hear June continue with her monologue about her teen prodigy. He is top of his class and she is going on and on about this kid in his class that is so disruptive. She says, "I don't understand why they let these kids with behavioral problems in the classroom. It only distracts the good kids from trying to learn." She continues to say, "If their parents cannot control them, then our kids should not be punished by others inability to parent."

"I know what I would do if that were my child," she states. "They would only act that way once before they learned the consequences. I can guarantee they wouldn't act that way

again. It's just not fair to the good kids," she said.

Lori feels the emotion rising up so she quickly excuses herself to go to the ladies room. As she is walking away, it takes all her strength to contain the tears. Her mind is swirling. Tommy now fits into the category of "the enemy of the good kids." Her aloneness is deafening and her emotions are a big bowl of "fruit basket turnover." June has no idea about life not being fair, she thinks to herself bitterly.

She finally returns to the table. She is still hurt to the core by June's comments and again has to fight the urge to just disappear. She feels another strong dose of embarrassment, shame, anger, guilt, failure, and ache to defend her son. He can't help his disability, she screams in her head. Should he be condemned to isolation so he will not bother the other kids? Is she a bad parent? Is this all her fault?

The tears are flowing when Robert gets home from work. Lori has been crying for at least an hour. Robert asked, "What's wrong?" She bursts out, "I just can't take it." "We just do not fit anywhere! I have to listen to mothers at work talk about their children and their "normal" worries and successes. They share their opinions about disruptive kids and inept parents. It is so painful. Why does it have to be so hard?"

I know Tommy can't help it, but it doesn't make it any easier. It feels like no matter where we go, I am being assaulted emotionally. The stares at the grocery store, listening to mothers' bragging about their "normal" lives, war zone at school, and the constant demands at home." Robert holds her and he fights back tears of his own.

She remembers the early years with Robert and the complications of a blended family. Robert continues to hug her. He reminds her of the hard times and the good times they've come through. "We have to keep our hope alive," he prods. "Without it, we have nothing." She knows he is right, but it is so hard when everyday is like being on the frontlines of a battlefield. The battlefield is in her homeland, in fact, in her very home and in her community.

Her faith is almost nonexistent these days. She has been praying for years for God to heal Tommy. At this point, she

*would just settle for some peace. Church is becoming
increasingly harder to attend because she never knows if Tommy
will act out, have a meltdown, or worse, be aggressive towards
someone. There are no special classes at church for him, and it
is difficult for him to sit through the whole service. But if she is
being really honest, she feels somewhat abandoned by God. It is
all just too much! People who aren't even in church or Christians
seem to have a better life than she does, she thinks.*

*The fight seems unending and she is battle fatigued. She
had not expected this would be a part of Tommy's diagnosis of
autism. She had no idea she would be battling her own private
war alongside him. She knows Robert is right. She can't give up,
but she is not sure how much longer she can hold on. He is
getting older and bigger...*

Lori's emotions are all over the map! Is it any wonder?
You may be reading this and thinking, no way something like this
could happen. There is no way someone would say something
like that principal did to that parent. YES! I have heard
countless stories, some worse than others, but the reality of
raising a child with special needs is it is often complicated. We
have conversations with others or situations occur that create
waves of emotional conflict for us to try to sort though.

We sometimes face emotional waves daily, hourly, or
minute by minute when we interact in our communities or with
family and friends. The onslaught can be overwhelming at times.

Offhanded statements such as "all the other parents
manage to get their kids here on time, your child should not be
given special treatment" can be hurtful. It may not be meant as
insensitive or personal towards you. It can feel personal when
you are doing the very best you can and feel unfairly judged.
These challenging statements can feel like one more weight piled
on top of an already too heavy load.

It could be a friend, doctor, coworker, teacher, or family
member that unintentionally says something that is insensitive,
diminishing, or invalidates your feelings of grief. Spoken words
can cause secondary psychological damage or trauma. Think
about what the principal said to Lori. She was already in crisis,

rushing to school to pick up Tommy, and the principal's words caused a secondary emotional trauma.

Remember Lori's experience with her coworker, June? Work conversations are commonly geared towards family. Topics such as their kids making honor roll, high scores on the ACT, getting their driver's license, first loves, show choir, sports, and all other forms of pride are all topics which parents love to share.

When you have a child with developmental disabilities, you have the same desire to brag and talk about your child that you love, but you may find the conversation hard to join because your child's goals or accomplishments are miles apart from typically developing kids. The conversations may be painful because they shine a spotlight on the delays or limitations of your child. It can leave you feeling disconnected and unable to fully relate. It can cause a sense of aloneness when surrounded by people.

Coworkers certainly mean no harm. Many of them are innocently bragging about their children. It is what parents do. Our reactions are a part of the A-typical Cyclic Grief response because we are living life outside the "normal" limits. We are constantly bombarded with the losses of what "should have been."

Soon after my son turned six, his father and I divorced. I was granted sole custody. My son never saw his biological father again after the divorce. It was a very complicated situation. I found myself a single parent of an amazing 6 year old. Both my son and I had been abandoned by his father.

A year or so later, I was at a social party talking with a group of people, both male and female. It was a rare occasion for me to get out, so I was enjoying my time. The subject of divorce came up. One of the women in our conversation circle was going through a divorce at that time. She knew I had a son with autism. She was talking about the challenges of her divorce and moving on. She looked at me, and in front of the entire group of people asked, "Aren't you afraid that no one will want you because you have a son with autism?"

She went on to say, "I worry about not being wanted

myself because of my age and having teenage daughters, but I would imagine not many people would want to take on the burden of a child with a disability like autism." I was dumbfounded!!

I was embarrassed, angry, humiliated, and hurt, just to name of few of the emotions that washed over me in that moment. Honestly, I loved my son so much and found him so adorable that it NEVER crossed my mind that he would be BAGGAGE! In fact, I really did not see myself ever getting married again, because I wasn't sure I would ever meet anyone capable of filling such big shoes as those of being his daddy.

I vowed to protect him as much as possible, for he had suffered enough for multiple lifetimes by the age of 6. I could not believe she asked such a question. She insinuated that he was unlovable, a liability, like some horrible disease! It took everything in me not to cry on the spot or reach out and tear her face off. Good thing I am not a violent person.

My eyes filled with tears as I immediately excused myself to use the ladies room. I was so upset, and all I could think of is how much I wanted to leave and go hug my precious little boy. That "burden" as she called him that rocked my world. That is just what I did. Her questions and comments left a negative impression on me, to say the least, and definitely caused secondary trauma.

If I were tracking and rating insensitive things that have been said to me over the years, her words would definitely rate in my top 10 for sure. I am still not sure to this day if her question was innocent or intentionally mean. Either way, as parents of children with a disability, we are bombarded with other people's words daily that trigger an emotional response. Even innocent words can still hurt.

You have probably heard the saying, "God gives special children to special parents." People say this as if God gave our children a disability as some special reward because we somehow deserve it. My child is a gift from God, but so are all children, disability or not. I do not believe God gives any child a disability. However, that topic is for another book.

I am convinced, for the most part; people are trying to

give us comfort and assurance but are just not sure how to go about it. So, they say things that are meant to make us feel special, proud, or "normal". We may experience emotional conflict when well meaning people give us sympathy. We want to feel understood and have our challenges recognized and validated by others, but sympathy can actually devalue our children.

In the South, people's hearts are blessed all the time. If someone is struggling, bless their heart. If someone doesn't understand, bless their heart. If they are unattractive, bless their hearts. So, when you are telling someone about your child and they say, "bless his heart," they mean it sympathetically, but it can also suggest they are somehow less than or pitiful.

We want our children to be accepted as equal in value, not seen as less than because of their disability. Our kids are not defined by their disability, they are affected by it. Their value is the same as any other human being. It is a tight wire! These sympathetic remarks are usually meant to be kind but it still stings at times nonetheless. I want to pause here to take a minute to try to see things from other people's view.

Your experiences and understanding of life outside of "normal" has given or will give you 20/20 vision into the realm of insensitive and inappropriate ways people living in "normal" respond to our situations. But we have to ask ourselves, "Without this insight we have, how would we respond?"

People strike up conversations based on the norms or average of the society in which they live. They expect "normal" and then don't know exactly what to say if it's abnormal. They say the wrong thing sometimes, perhaps judge too quickly, or try to avoid you altogether. Ask yourself, "If my child was "normal" and I didn't know what I know now, what would I say or do?" There is no way to truly know the answer, but if we are honest, maybe we would be among the masses doing it wrong. Honestly, it may not make the insensitive words hurt less, but we can't expect someone who's never driven in snow or ice to know that you don't hit the brakes on icy roads. This kind of knowledge comes through experience. Just try to keep that in mind. It might make it easier to forgive or overlook the insensitivities we are destined to encounter.

Western culture also plays a part in contributing to our emotional turmoil. In the United States, the focus is always on the ability of the child with the disability. You probably have all heard the catchphrases such as dis "ability" or "what is normal anyway?" There are the touching stories about good Samaritans that show kindness to our children or human triumph that makes us all feel good. This is good! We should focus on our child's abilities and strengths.

Focusing on abilities is not the problem. The problem is focusing on ability while ignoring the complex emotional issues faced by parents and sometimes the child. I would guess that your emotional experience with raising a child with a developmental disability is rarely, if ever, asked about in social settings. Most people are unsure of what to ask and you may be unsure of what to say. Our grief remains hidden as a result.

Think about it this way. It is common and caring for people to ask someone who has lost a loved one how he/she is doing emotionally and offer support. When was the last time someone asked you how you were handling the loss of "normal" and all the challenges of raising a child with a developmental disability? We grieve in silence.

It's almost like we feel shame if we talk about the loss of "normal" surrounding a child with a disability. As a result, we don't talk about it and people don't ask. It's a tidy little arrangement. What others don't understand is our children are not our source of grief. Rather it is the loss of "normal" caused by the disability. Trying to make a square peg fit into a round hole is exhausting.

We get that life will be different when we find out our child has a disability. We may not know how different or to what degree but we know it will not be what we expected. Learning to be okay with being different and the loss of the expected "normal" takes time and experience. Grief is not something to be bypassed but something to walk through. Emerging on the other side, stronger and content with our new normal makes it worth the walk. Take a few minutes to reflect on the following questions.

<u>Challenge Questions:</u>

1. What insensitive things have been said to you?

2. How did you handle those statements?

3. What are your daily challenges? Judgment from others? Stares? Your child's behavior?

4. How have you reacted to sympathy? How do you feel about sympathy?

5. Do you struggle with conversations at work? Do you hide your feelings?

6. How do you think your understanding is different since becoming a parent of a child with a disability?

7. Imagine the things you might say or do had you never had this experience. Would you be different? What would you want explained to you to help you understand?

8. Describe the emotional conflict you have experienced or may currently be experiencing.

9. What feelings do you encounter in your waves of emotion? Guilt? Anger? Resentment? Jealousy? Defensiveness? Protectiveness? Shame? Love? Isolation?

10. How can you reframe your experience through the eyes of others to give them more grace for their lack of understanding?

Remember: Emotional conflict describes the daily grief encounters. Learning to work through those encounters will help you face each day with a new perspective.

Chapter 11: Cave Dwelling

Hot and muggy; summer in the south is like living inside an invisible dome that creates a steam room effect. The air is thick and humid. It would be a perfect day for the pool instead of the first day of high school, she thinks. Lori couldn't believe her little blonde angel was so grown up. High school, she sighs. He still looks so handsome with his green eyes and olive complexion. His hair has become a dirtier blonde like hers since he has gotten older. Ninth grade! How is it possible, she wonders?

She remembers the little 3 year old that loved to play chase and giggle. The little boy that was more like an architect or audio recorder than a 3 year old, uniquely different. Even then, he was with me, yet lost in some vast space of brilliance and blankness all at the same time, she recalls. His is a crazy upside down world of sights and sounds that keeps him just out of reach of this world, only allowing him brief visits on occasion. Glimpses of "normal", the thought sparks hope and fuels despair. Her eyes fill as emotions flood her soul. My little boy, my teenager, my soon to be man, but nothing is as it should be.

Summer was pretty good as summers go, no aggression, a nice break for all of them. She is nervous about the return to school. Tommy has a personal aide that stays with him all day at school, and this year it is a newbie. Even though the new aide has received some training over the summer, the thought makes Lori cringe. Every time there is someone new, there is always a learning curve. Aggressive behaviors leave little room for a learning curve, she acknowledges. A sense of dread settles on her at the thought.

The middle school years have been much more difficult than she ever imagined they would be. Maybe high school will be better, she hopes and prays. He looks so striking in his new clothes against his tan skin. He is so attractive. She is sure a few of the girls would have had crushes on him if he had not been born with autism. The thought makes her sad somewhere deep inside, like the feeling you get when your heart has been broken. She still wonders what his life would have been like had he been "normal." Good-looking, smart, funny, athletic, she will never know. She loves him as he is and tries to focus on who he is, instead of what could have been, but still the sadness sits there like an elephant in the center of her life that she is constantly trying to ignore.

Tommy is standing in front of the fire place for his annual first day of school picture, looking annoyed because she is insisting on the shot. His smile looks more like he is ready to bite someone, but she learned long ago it is his best attempt at smiling for the camera, so she simply snaps the picture. They pile into the car and drive the short distance to school. Lori gets out so she can greet his new aide Ms. Ford. She seems pleasant enough and smiles eagerly at Tommy. Lori shares some highlights about Tommy that she believes will help the aide on her first day with him.

Tommy is excited and eager to start his day as well. She pulls away from school, knowing she will be on pins and needles all day hoping the phone will not ring. It didn't. Several hours later, she pulls up to the school to pick him up. She sees Tommy and his aide walking towards the car. They are both smiling. Relief washes over Lori. Tommy is talking to himself, but laughing all the while, so she knows it has been a good day. She asks him questions about school when he gets in the car, but gets the usual one word responses or garbled phrases that did not make much sense.

She and Robert had spent many hours over the summer working with the school and a behavioral specialist to come up with a plan to manage Tommy's behavior. His behavior was so challenging last year, they wanted to get ahead of the game this year and be better prepared. A plan was developed to prevent aggression and also address how to react should he become aggressive.

His aggression has never been premeditated or with intent to harm but rather reactionary to his environment, which is common in his disability of autism. She feels a little more confident this year with the specialist they brought in over the summer because of his vast knowledge. He wants Tommy to learn how to interact with others and learn proper behavior through a social learning approach. Lori smiles, as she reflects *on how much she has had to learn just to understand the lingo of the world of autism. In the beginning, it was like learning a foreign language. Now, it's like her second language, she muses.*

The specialist wants the aide to ignore any bad behavior but recognize and reward all good behavior. The approach is supposed to motivate Tommy to do more of the good behavior and less of the bad. The new aide has been trained on how to follow the plan. She appeared enthusiastic about her new job and working with Tommy, at least during the training over the summer, Lori reflects.

Tommy usually has very bad reactions if he is told "no" or scolded. He typically doesn't understand why he is being told no and instead of asking or arguing like most teens, his reaction tends to be more physical. He doesn't have the language ability to ask or argue in typical ways. He is eager to please and compliant most of the time. He loves being praised. In a weird way, it's like his emotional reactions are more on the level of a three year old than a teenager. Autism is complicated and hard to understand, even for her at times, she thinks as she replays it all in her head.

The specialist wrote into his school plan that he was not to be told no or scolded but simply ignored and rewarded. Because he doesn't fully comprehend or process verbal explanations, the specialist thought this approach would be the most effective way to teach him appropriate behavior and stop the aggressive reactions. The school agreed and trained everyone that would be interacting with Tommy throughout the school day, including teachers. She remembers feeling very grateful for the specialist and the school's willingness to follow the plan. Maybe this year will be better, she whispers quietly.

Today was a good day, she thinks. Perhaps the new aide will not have a huge learning curve, she hopes. Her mind shifts back to the present as she pulls in the driveway on their way home from school. As soon as Tommy came through the door, he headed to his room for some down time. Lori smiles, at least some things are still very predictable, she mumbles.

The next few days pass quickly, bringing the first week of school to an end. Lori parks in her usual place, enjoying the beautiful Friday weather as she waits for Tommy. She sees Ms. Ford approaching her vehicle, holding her arm, and she is not smiling. Tommy looks agitated. Lori asks what happened, and Ms. Ford informs her that she had to tell Tommy "no" and he pushed her. She said she thought her arm would be okay but she wasn't positive. Lori's heart sank. Why did you have to tell him no, she asks? Lori wasn't upset, just curious. "Because he needed to be told no," Ms. Ford snaps.

So much for the learning curve, Lori thought. Here we go again! She felt horrible for Ms. Ford but also worried. Something seemed cold about her today. Plus, Lori thought, she has been specifically trained to avoid using the word no; we talked for hours about it over the summer. Why?, Lori wondered, would she do that when she has been told in advance that it typically causes an aggressive reaction. She seemed angry today that he got aggressive, instead of expecting the aggression and responding the way she has been trained to handle it.

Lori doesn't want to complain or get Ms. Ford in trouble, because she has learned over the years it is best to keep a good working relationship with the people who will care for her son all day. She is also aware that school has just begun and it will take a little time to get in the groove of things. She decides not to say anything and remain positive.

Monday morning Lori sees Ms. Ford's arm in a sling as she drops Tommy off and her heart skips a beat. Her stomach does a few flips at the overwhelming sense of fear that grips her. Something feels wrong. Still nothing is said, not by Lori or Ms. Ford. Lori asks Ms. Ford if her arm is broken or if she tore anything internally. Ms. Ford abruptly says, "No, but the doctor thought it would be a good idea to wear the sling, just to rest it because it is sore." Lori immediately gets an image of someone in a neck brace suing for damages. Something doesn't feel right about this, she thinks. But, then she guesses she is just being paranoid.

The weeks go by ushering in fall, always a welcomed season in their household. Robert loves football and the cooler weather. Tommy loves to go camping, especially with his favorite aunt and uncle, mainly because he can eat junk food such as s'mores. She and Robert are doing pretty well as a couple but both are worried about Tommy and school. Tommy is more negative since school started back, even at home. Even though nothing has been reported by the school, it is a sign that something is off. She tries to pry information out of Tommy but it's useless.

They have seen the doctor so frequently over the past few years, since the aggression started, trying this medication or that one, always looking for something that might settle the aggression. Sometimes it feels like a rollercoaster ride stuck in motion, she thinks, or like they are chasing rabbits. The psychiatric nurse practitioner has, at times, been a regular phone call each week for Lori. The doctors assure her that Tommy will get better and grow out of the aggression at some point.

Tommy is considered moderately autistic. He is not severe by definition, but he is not mild either, at least that's the way the doctor explained it. Moderates tend to have more communication troubles and aggression is not uncommon, at least through puberty and adolescence, according to the specialist. Yep, she can definitely confirm that is true, at least for Tommy. When will this get easier, she wonders? Adolescence can last beyond 20 years old; the thought sends electric shock waves down her spine. She is tired of this emotional rollercoaster. The guilt she feels every time she hands her child a handful of pills is overwhelming at times.

Since that first week of school, there have not been any more reports of aggression and she is very grateful. Even though things seem to be relatively stable at school, Lori still has a bad feeling about Ms. Ford. It feels like the giant is sleeping, soon to wake angry and ready to wage war. It is an impending sense of doom.

This is the first time she has ever felt this way about an aid, and it is freaking her out. Tommy has had numerous aides throughout the years, all with different personalities, but none gave Lori the eerie feeling that Ms. Ford does. She prays silently asking God to protect Tommy, but struggles to hide her doubt that he will honor her request. Does God hear me or care, she wonders. Her heart sinks.

She feels distant, untrusting, and isolated, even from God these days. It's another loss. How can she trust that God will protect Tommy from Ms. Ford if he hasn't protected him from autism? She looks around and sees all these people with their perfect lives that talk about God's favor. Worse are those who brag about God blessing them with healthy children. I guess that means God did not bless me, she thinks bitterly. She still believes in God but has lost hope that anything will really change. The sobering thoughts strike fear and sorrow in her soul.

Early spring arrives, ushering in Lori's favorite time of year. She loathes winter and lives for summers. Spring is like the gateway to summer, at least in her mind. It's mid March and her feelings of impending doom have grown into a deep concern bordering on anxiety and panic. Ms. Ford has gone from being cold to actually giving Lori dirty looks from behind school doors when she arrives to pick Tommy up from school. She looks as if she hates Tommy. Tommy does not seem to care much for her either. He isn't unkind; it is simply not in his nature. He tries to warm up to her, but her body language says it all. She is just not interested and Tommy senses it.

He is agitated most days and generally not happy when she picks him up. Lori is gravely concerned. Something in her gut is firing off warning signals; something is wrong. What is it, she wonders? She decides to trust her instinct and meet with the high school principal. He is an older man set to retire this year. Lori has worked with him for several years now and she has grown to trust and respect him very much. He is warm, genuine, and caring by her assessment. His demeanor and approach is in stark contrast to the middle school principal. She is grateful for the differences.

During her meeting with the principal, she asked him to talk with Ms. Ford. If she was even the slightest bit uncomfortable working with Tommy, Lori requested to have her reassigned. She knows that autism is complicated and the behaviors can be extremely difficult to understand. She shared all of her concerns with the principal but also made sure he understood that she realizes not everyone is cut out to work with kids with autism. Maybe it is more than the aide bargained for, *and they should give her the chance to move. The principal agreed.*

Lori was told later, by the principal, that Ms. Ford said she was not uncomfortable and did not need to be reassigned when he had spoken with her. She was relieved the principal had spoken with Ms. Ford. It made her feel slightly better, but it didn't explain the dirty looks and unease that Lori continues to experience. Is it in my head, Lori questions? Have I misread the looks? She hopes so. At least it has been addressed and the new aide has been given a way out if she is unhappy.

Tommy started vocational school in the afternoons this semester for part of his high school experience. The vocational school is a 45 minute drive from the high school. Ms. Ford rides the bus with him and assists him while he is there. So far, things have gone well, as far as Lori knows. She has not been told otherwise. Ms. Ford is supposed to report any aggressive behavior to Lori and Tommy's special education case manager at school. She assumes everything is fine, but the dread never leaves. The thoughts and fears that something is wrong never leave. Is this some sort of post traumatic stress left over from last year, she wonders? Maybe it's all me.

As the end of the year is approaching, Tommy is more negative than ever, but still no aggressive behaviors have been reported. In fact, nothing good or bad has been shared with her. She feels completely out of the loop. She has to rely on the people at school to tell her about Tommy's day because he is not able. He mimics or repeats things others say in front of him, like the tape recorder he resembled back in preschool. Only now, it is hard to tell who is saying what.

He still watches Disney movies quite a bit and seems to identify with the villains when he is upset or as a way to show his displeasure. He talks about KoCoum a lot, which is an Indian character from the movie Pocahontas. KoCoum was a very angry Indian who tried to choke John Smith because he thought he was taking Pocahontas away. The phone rang. It was early afternoon and the caller ID showed the call coming from the trade school. Lori's heart sank! It was the principal of the vocational school, and she told Lori to come get Tommy right away, because there had been an incident. She told her Tommy was okay but she needed to get there as soon as possible.

Lori immediately dove in the car, driving faster than she should have to get to Tommy. When she arrived, the first person she saw when she walked in the front door was Ms. Ford, and this time, she was holding her neck. Oh no!, she thought. She asks her if she is okay, but she does not answer her, she just looks the other way.

The principal of the vocational school approached Lori and told her to take Tommy home and she would call her the next day to talk about the incident. She asked the principal what happened, but she told her to just tend to Tommy and she would be told about the incident later. She knew in her gut the situation would not be good.

She took her son to the car and asked him what happened, knowing he would only be able to give her fragments. Judging from the look on his face, he was visibly shaken. He said he was being Kocoum, trying to rescue him from Ms. Ford. He frequently mixed up his pronouns and referred to himself in third person. She knew he was trying to say that he was rescuing himself because he felt threatened in some way. She also knew Kocoum choked his nemesis.

She consoled herself by remembering that when she saw Ms. Ford she was walking around and talking with other teachers. Although she did not speak to Lori, she observed her laughing and carrying out duties like nothing had happened. Calm down, she chides herself. Ms. Ford is perfectly fine.

She was fighting the urge to go straight home and never leave the house again. She can't keep this up! It feels like it never stops. She looks over at her teenage son, struggling to hold back the tears. He is a very young child trapped in a teenage body. His innocence is still remarkable. He doesn't even know about the birds and the bees yet. She loves him so much and feels a strong urge to protect him. He isn't even able to tell her exactly what happened and why he looks so scared and upset.

Her mind wonders about the fallout. She imagined it would be a suspension from school, and they would have to revisit the behavioral plan. She has so many questions unanswered. How and why did this happen? All Tommy keeps saying is "She's bad" "She's taking him away" "She's mad" "Kocoum protected him." That helps a lot, she whispers sarcastically. She is worried about Ms. Ford. It was obvious she was okay physically but surely it had to have been upsetting. She had not been injured, thank God!

Silently she whispers, God where are you? She can't remember another time she has ever felt so distant and abandoned by God. All the messages of years past play through her mind. God heals all our sickness, He will direct your path, He will work all things for your good, He will make a way, and He can do the impossible. She is at a loss. Why me? Why my little boy?

Realizing that her thoughts are full of questions left unanswered, she feels surrounded by the unknown. A foreign land with no maps or signs to follow, a desolate road revealing miles of nothingness, in a car with a flashing light warning low fuel. Utter loss and disappointment with a splash of fear, she acknowledges. She is afraid of her own thoughts but she feels powerless to find her way out of this emotional tunnel her life is plowing through. She has to keep it together, she reminds herself. Poker face! The thought brings a cynical smirk to her lips.

It's almost laughable how well she hides this private storm she fights every day, except from Robert. Her co-workers have no idea of the emotional battlefield she winds her way through every single day. She is ashamed to tell people the truth. She believes deep down she will be judged harshly, or worse, Tommy will be judged!

Lori was crying when Robert came home from work. She told him about the incident and her fears. Lori was calming down just as the phone rang. She answered; it was the principal of the high school. He said, "Ms. Jones, I'm sorry to be the one to tell you this, but I really felt like you had the right to know." "The District Attorney called me today to inform me that they are moving forward with felony charges against Tommy for assaulting Ms. Ford." Lori couldn't breathe. She couldn't speak.

He went on, "Ms. Ford went to the hospital this evening

on her own time after school hours and pressed charges against Tommy while she was at the hospital." She told the police she has been keeping a private journal about his aggressive behavior everyday and wants him charged. WHAT? A journal, charges, a FELONY, how is this possible? Do they know he is autistic?, she asks the principal. Lori begins to panic. It feels like the room is closing in on her. This can't be real.

He was a kind and honest man. Lori could tell he was upset and worried for Tommy just as she was. He told her he tried to convince the DA that pressing charges against Tommy is a mistake and inappropriate due to his level of disability, but the DA refused to listen and was moving forward anyway based on Ms. Ford's report. Why would she keep a private journal Lori asks? Confusion, shock, and fear grip at her soul, and she fights back panic waiting for his answer.

The principal informed her that he had spoken with the school attorney as well, and learned that Ms. Ford had hired an attorney. "It looks like she is planning to sue the school, and possibly you as well, for punitive damages," he said. "It's about money?", Lori gasps at the realization, as her mind flashes over all the dirty looks, the sling, and her constant sense that something was wrong. This can't be happening! Lori is dazed and confused. With tears in her eyes and fear in her heart, she hands the phone over to Robert to take over the conversation. She had no more words.

Her head was spinning and her mind was a constant reel of panic. Is Tommy going to jail? Are they coming to pick him up? Oh my Lord, he will be so scared! He doesn't even understand any of this! She started crying. Please God! Please protect Tommy, she cried, this time replacing doubt with desperation.

Lori felt more alone than she had ever felt in her life. Just when she thought things couldn't be worse, boy was she wrong. She felt violated for Tommy and couldn't help but feel like it was all about MONEY! This woman hid his behavior from all of us so she could secretly build a case against an autistic teenager. Punitive damage equals money, plain and simple. The motive was clear, at least to Lori. She doesn't care about what happens to Tommy. She doesn't care if it is at his expense. The dirty looks, cold stares, the sling, all the memories flood Lori's mind again. No wonder warning sirens were going off about Ms. Ford.

Lori didn't know what to do. She was completely powerless to protect her child. Her only hope was something greater than her. She could not do this without God. Fear made her look up, even though she still felt abandonment; she knows God is her only hope, her only source of peace in the middle of this raging storm. She was desperate! *God forgive me and please help us*, she prayed in a barely audible voice.

A few weeks passed and Lori learned that Tommy would not be picked up by the police. She was finally given a copy of the journal kept by Ms. Ford. Lori could not believe the contents. This woman actually wrote in her journal that she thought Tommy knew exactly what he was doing and was just a bad kid who had been spoiled his entire life. In other words, *he doesn't have a disability, he is just unruly. He is just pretending to not be able to communicate, he just pretends to talk to himself, he is faking autism;* Lori jeers under her breath.

It seemed to Lori that Ms. Ford thought her knowledge was superior to the vast number of specialists involved in Tommy's diagnosis and care over the years. The aide wrote about how ridiculous it was that he was not supposed to be told no. She wrote about his bad behavior all day long, no matter what he was doing, as if he was under a microscope all day. Lori wondered how in the world she ever had time to help Tommy with anything in light of all the entries. She knew the answer. She didn't help him; she was simply building a lawsuit for an entire year. The thought made Lori outraged.

The aide's own accounts provided evidence that she had not been following the behavior plan set up by the specialist. Not even loosely. Poor Tommy! Lori could only imagine what his days must have been like with Ms. Ford. No wonder he had become so negative!

There were dates in the journal where the aide reported that Tommy had said or done things. However, these were dates where he was absent from school. The most remarkable thing

Lori noticed was the absence of anything positive. She did not have one kind word for Tommy in her journal. Not one. For an entire year, she filled pages with hateful words. If she did not have anything bad to write about him, she wrote nothing. Blank pages meant a good day.

She had been building a case, according to her journal, since that first week of school when he pushed her after she told him no. She lied to the principal about being comfortable with Tommy. The journal was evidence she was Tommy's prosecutor rather than his helper. She was never comfortable with him. She loathed him based on her journal contents. It seemed clear to Lori the reason she didn't want to be moved is because she needed the continued data for her lawsuit. This is a nightmare, of a sinister nature, Lori thought.

When all the facts came out about the day at the vocational school, it was reported that Ms. Ford had taken Tommy outside the building at trade school through a side door, the only door with a broken camera. A remote side door, nonetheless not the front doors where others would be around if she needed support. None of the interactions between Tommy and Ms. Ford outside the building were witnessed by anyone or caught on camera. Why would she take him to a remote location alone if she was claiming that he was upset and needed to be taken out of the room? Her journal states numerous times she was fearful of him. Why would she do that when we had already agreed that the teacher would take over? Why would someone who is afraid of someone take him/her to a remote location alone if he/she is becoming agitated? Lori wondered. It just doesn't make sense! It reminds her of Robert's ex-wife and the professional that tried to use Tommy's disability for personal gain.

Lori was livid that nothing was being done by the school system about Ms. Ford. She had been moved to another student immediately, but she was still working at the school. None of it made sense. Lori felt like she should have been put on administrative leave at a minimum. She had also been made aware that Ms. Ford was suing the school, so she wondered if that tied their hands.

They assigned a new aide to Tommy but Ms. Ford was still at the same school, so every day she felt a pit in her stomach when she dropped Tommy off at school. It was a heart wrenching time in her life. She didn't know who to trust and Tommy couldn't tell her how he was being treated or what was being said to him. She really liked the new young man working with Tommy and felt very comfortable with him. Nothing like she felt with Ms. Ford. Still everything was uncertain. She felt a new tension or awkwardness with the school.

The fear of the unknown, in light of the felony charges, is a daily panic deep in her heart. She feels so alone but afraid to tell anyone, even her closest friends, about the incident. After all, no matter what the truth is, felony charges are a hard sell when attempting to generate feelings of compassion. Robert is at her side and Tommy's, but it feels like it's them against the world, a position she is becoming well acquainted with by now. She has always been a fighter and a social butterfly but these later years have changed her. She has little fight left and the last thing she wants to be is social. She can just imagine the party conversations. No thank you, she thinks.

She feels depression creeping in and isn't sure she has the strength to fight back. What's next? She is crippled by the fear of what the future will bring...

I would often have days when I first began to cycle through the grief that I wished I could just be a cave dweller. The idea of either living alone on an island with my son or in a cave somewhere was very appealing. At least I could love and accept him. If he threw the mother of all tantrums, I could just plug my ears and let him go at it. If he talked to himself loudly for hours on end, I was cool with that. It was his way of winding down. But unfortunately, those behaviors were not as accepted in the larger community outside of our home, and I knew it. My feelings of isolation and wanting to take my son far away where he could be himself without judgment went unnoticed by those around me. The silent grief continued.

Lori's situation is grim and challenging. Hopefully, many of you have not experienced such dire circumstances but I fear that some of you may. Regardless of the level of difficulty, we all feel at times that life would just be simpler if we could be left alone in our own normal. Your normal may be a few miles or many miles apart from the "normal" you expected. Distance is distance. It still leaves you feeling isolated.

The difficulties surrounding our life may cause us to choose avoidance rather than facing more emotional trauma. Others may not take into account the battles some of us face simply getting our children to the car, much less to an appointment or school. I have heard many parents talk about the battles that they encounter with their children over clothing, food, showers, and so on, all prior to the school day.

Just like Lori, routine life stuff such as going to the grocery store, school activities, church, and sporting events can become hard to endure. This can be especially true with children who have behavioral outbursts, running away behaviors, or other maladaptive behaviors that make interactions outside the home extremely difficult. Over time, it can cause you to feel like a misfit. You can lose your sense of belonging in our society.

It sounds like a recipe for cave dwelling if you ask me. Seriously, it can be overwhelming and cause us to choose aloneness rather than social interaction. Think about Lori in her younger years. She was very social with lots of friends. Life has become so complicated for her; it is just easier to stay home. Have you ever felt that way? Can you identify with Lori? I certainly have at times throughout my journey.

Here's a quote from an article that really stuck with me over the years. "What has taken place when a child is diagnosed with a disability? A personal, quiet tragedy for a parent and a child has transpired, but, in the absence of a physical death to mourn, it has no prescribed rituals for parents or others" (Bruce & Schultz, 2002).

The quote is from an article in the British Journal of Special Education about nonfinite loss and challenges to communication between parents and professionals. Think about this quote. Try to digest it. The author is recognizing that the loss of "normal" is real but our society does not know how to respond to the loss. He was totally on track, in my opinion. This is why I think Lori and perhaps many of us don't talk about it. We instinctively fear people will not know what to say, because we don't know what to say. Silent grief leads to isolation.

Imagine how different you might have felt if others would have called you and offered support once they learned your child had been diagnosed with a disability. What if they would have talked to you about the loss of "normal" and the stages of A-typical Cyclic Grief? What if they had told you what to expect? What if they would have validated your feelings and encouraged you to embrace your new normal? What if they could have told you about others that share your new journey and have learned to love their new normal? Wow! I wish I could have had that experience.

We all face embarrassing or humiliating moments involving our kids that highlight the lack of awareness of others. I remember the time we were sitting in a restaurant eating dinner when my son was around age 11. He had been learning about health in school. He had also picked up a few words from school to describe various body types. These were not words we used in my household. An overweight man walked by our booth and my 11 year old son blurted out "He's fat." I nearly choked on my food. I looked at the man who repaid my glance with a dirty look. I get it. If he had been three years old rather than eleven, the man would have been much more forgiving. But, an eleven year old speaking in that manner, that is just poor parenting.

After that embarrassing encounter, I spent a great deal of time trying to teach my son that we do not use words like "fat" or "skinny" etc. I told him how it could make people feel bad. I decided we would do our own health study at home. My son was slightly overweight himself, so I thought that it would be a great opportunity to talk about healthy versus unhealthy, being mindful to avoid terms such as skinny or fat. It worked! My son had lost a few pounds and was able to recognize healthy weight from unhealthy weight.

The following year, while on vacation, we had just arrived at a water park. We were all in our swimsuits and very excited for a day of fun. We got out of our car and began our jog towards the entrance. Just in front of us are two very curvy women. I hear my son yell from behind me. "Whoa!" I turned to see him pointing at these two women within 15 feet of us and I'm pretty sure I stopped breathing.

He announced in the loudest voice you can imagine. Seriously, it was like he had a megaphone. "Look mom, they are really UNHEALTHY!" My face turned at least 50 shades of red. Both women had turned to hear his announcement and it was obvious, by their faces, they did not appreciate his declaration. I was mortified! He meant no harm. He was merely making an observation, at least in his mind. He was proud that he had become so healthy. My son did not look like he had a disability, so the women looked like they were either going to come after him or me. I suddenly remembered I forgot something in the car.

I am sure many of you have had moments such as these that perhaps you laugh at now. It's better than crying. I really wanted to apologize to both of the women but I was too afraid. My son certainly fell into the category of saying and doing things that were outside the "normal" limits, which brought judgment from others. Sometimes we could predict what he was going to say or how he would react, but other times, it was like Christmas morning, you never knew what you were going to get.

These experiences, both the humorous and non humorous, are added incidents that we have to deal with, and sometimes frequently, depending on the child. The non humorous events can leave us wiped out emotionally. I don't know about you, but I have felt completely isolated right in the middle of a sea of people. Just because we have people around us does not mean we do not feel alone sometimes. We all need to be able to share our feelings without fear of judgment from others. Avoiding pain and difficulty is a natural human instinct but it can often lead to isolation if the pain we try to avoid occurs when interacting with others.

The quote mentioned earlier by Bruce & Schultz 2002, talks about a set of prescribed rituals that people follow when they recognize that someone has experienced a loss. Think about the benefits of having such a ritual that would provide guidance on how to understand our journey and give us the support we need when we are figuring out how to deal with the loss of normal developmental functioning in our children. It would be similar to teaching proper etiquette, wouldn't it be great. Perhaps breaking the silence barrier will be a start. We can help people understand our experiences. Knowledge is power. Changing mindsets and stigmas are important. Yes, we do grieve and it is a natural part of the process, but we adore our children as well.

Perhaps we can learn to reach out instead of isolating. We can talk about our feelings without shame because they will be better understood. The loner approach is completely understandable but isolation only leads to depression in time. Even though the reasons for just staying home and away from everyone are valid, you have to remind yourself that it has to have a time limit. We all need someone! Remember the song "We all need somebody to lean on…" It is true. My hope is we can begin to talk openly about this topic and encourage one another in support groups, friend groups, and families across the nation. Isolation and lack of support can lead to depression. Take some time to answer the following questions.

Challenge Questions:

1. **Have you isolated from the world around you?**

2. **Has your lifestyle changed? Your friend group?**

3. **Do you feel disconnected from those around you even when you are in large group gatherings?**

4. **Do you feel unfairly judged by others?**

5. **Are there any support groups in your local area?**

6. **Will you commit to reaching out to connect with others who share your journey?**

Remember: Avoidance and time alone make sense at times, but if it becomes a lifestyle, it will lead to depression or other unhealthy outcomes. You are NOT ALONE!

Chapter 12: Eeyore Days.

She barely had the energy to drag herself out of bed today. She has been sleeping a lot lately and just letting Tommy do his own thing. After the school system pressed their own set of charges against him to try to push him out of school, Lori caved. He now faces two counts of felony class C or B, she can't remember. Let's add in a misdemeanor, disturbing the peace, and a few others that she can't recall either.

She reflects back on how bad things had become at school for Tommy. The school board attorney became involved and the school kept Tommy isolated based on the attorney's advisement. They would not let him eat or even be in the restroom at the same time as the other kids. Wow, I guess June is not the only one who thinks these kids should just be taken out of circulation, she thinks bitterly.

The kids had always liked Tommy and he liked them. He was social, like Lori. The isolation was cruel. Tommy had never hit another student and was not a threat. The lawsuit by Ms. Ford had everyone scared.

The isolation was a result of the incident with Ms. Ford. Lori remembers being on pins and needles every day fearing what the school would do if another incident occurred. The likelihood of an incident was definitely high, because, after all, he has autism and very poor communication skills.

What was she supposed to do? Save the world from her son or fight to help her son? It felt like a rock and a hard place. She felt like the villain in either scenario. Tommy was being punished and he had no one but her to fight for him, so her role was clear.

She was trying to make them do the right thing and allow Tommy to go back to the trade school. Pull him out of isolation. Stop this madness. She had hired a school attorney to represent Tommy. It was as if they were punishing Tommy for what Ms. Ford had done. The tragedy is, she continues to work with other children, with no consequences for her lies and manipulation. The school system actually tried to use her journal as a record of Tommy's behavior but Tommy's school attorney got it thrown out.

The trade school battle was ridiculous, she reflects, still lost in her own thoughts. The school had brought in their own specialist again, the one from last year. The school was hoping he would say that Tommy should not be allowed to go back to the trade school because of his behavior and should be kept in isolation. It backfired on them. He stated, in writing, that Tommy should be returned to trade school immediately, as it is the most appropriate education for him and his behaviors should be addressed through a behavior plan.

The specialist openly noted the negligence of Ms. Ford and her egregious failure to follow the behavior plan as being a factor in Tommy's behavior. He also said the isolation was cruel and unjustified. He talked about the importance of Tommy being around other students. The school didn't budge. They refused to let him attend trade school and kept him in isolation. They brought in another specialist that had never worked with Tommy before, again hoping for different recommendations, but again were defeated by their own actions.

The new specialist was essentially a repeat of the first. This new specialist went on to say that his behaviors were not outside of the norm for teens with autism and should be managed through a behavior plan. She confirmed that he should be placed back at trade school immediately and with other students, because it was the most appropriate place for him to learn. The school would not budge. They hired yet another specialist who confirmed the same recommendations as the first two. Still, they would not budge.

She remembers her decision to take them to court after she realized they were not going to relent. It was a hard decision but she felt like she had no other choice, because her son needed to be in trade school and with other students, just like the specialists all had recommended. It was baffling to her that the school would not follow the recommendations of the people they hired.

The hearing date was set and ironically, it was just days away, when Tommy had his next meltdown at school. It seemed to be perfect timing for the school system. Her greatest fear came to life with a vengeance. Something happened that caused a meltdown. It was nothing serious compared to past meltdowns, but in light of the criminal charges, everything had become serious.

This time he threw something while he was in the principal's office. He did not put his hands on anyone, thank goodness, and no students were around to witness the meltdown. The high school principal, the one Lori respected, had retired last year and was replaced by the former middle school principal. The meltdown occurred in his office.

The day it occurred he had told Lori to take Tommy home and that everything was fine. The next day, charges were filed by that same principal. She remembers the shock she felt when she learned he had not only suspended her son but pressed criminal charges against him. The nightmare worsened.

The principal stated he had been hit by a tiny piece of glass that had broken off of the thrown object, so he filed assault charges against Tommy. Lori had spent an hour with him the day it occurred, and he had told her about the piece of glass, stating it was "no big deal because it did not injure him in any way." Apparently, he changed his mind and story. Tommy's attorneys had received the police report and they had notified Lori.

Lori was suspicious that maybe the principal had been forced to press charges by the school board and their attorney. She believed that he had not planned to take any actions, just as he had said that day in his office. Maybe she was being too generous by giving him the benefit of the doubt, but she also knew that somewhere along the way, the school that she had trusted to help her with Tommy had become the enemy.

The school wanted Tommy out. Bottom line, he had become too much of a nuisance and they were going to do everything in their power to push him out. At least, this is how it appeared to Lori. The criminal attorneys representing Tommy said they believed the charges were intended to make Lori back down as well. They were trying to intimidate her by making his melt-downs a criminal offense.

In her way of thinking, it seemed they had made it illegal to have autism or behaviors that are common in autism. Apply pressure where it counts and she will cave, seemed to be their strategy. They were right. She did. She withdrew him from that school system and transferred him to a home school program. Home school has been a huge relief. They could get their hours in however they wanted or needed because the home school covering was designed for kids with special needs. He was not isolated anymore.

Robert's brother was an attorney who referred them to the current criminal attorney who was now defending Tommy. In fact, he and his colleague both wanted to represent Tommy. They were outraged by the charges and wanted to set a precedent. With all these charges, they have plenty to work with, she thinks sarcastically. It just keeps piling on.

The civil suit for punitive damages attempted by Ms. Ford went nowhere. She learned early on that she could not sue the school system and she could not sue Lori for anything that happened while Tommy was in the care of the school. The year's worth of planning on her behalf turned out to be a dead end street. The thought gives Lori some sense of justice.

Her mind shifts back into the present. It's D-Day. Tommy will meet his probation officer for the first time. The realization of Tommy having a probation officer is ludicrous. It is like someone wrote a satire of their lives and they are following the script.

She has definitely learned that the court system is slow as molasses. It has taken months just to get to this point. She is also learning more about criminal law than she ever thought she would. This should be a sight, she imagines, as she pictures the meeting between Tommy and the probation officer. Negativity and a cynical outlook are constant companions of hers these days. It is just all so over the top. It never seems to let up. She is irritable, fatigued, hopeless, shameful, sleeping all the time, and has no energy. Depression is taking up full time residency and she doesn't even care at this point. She forces herself to get dressed because Robert is coming home from work so he can go with them.

Robert is helping Tommy get ready and trying to explain to him what a parole officer is and what to expect, which is *laughable, because we do not know what to expect ourselves. An hour later, they pull into the courthouse parking lot and Lori is overcome with emotions. She is trying to hide her fear from her son. It feels surreal. This is not the place for him. This is so wrong, she thinks.*

Walking into the courthouse, going through metal detectors, police officers standing by, are all amazing to Tommy, who still does not comprehend what is going on. Tony, the parole officer, was a polite young man who seemed just as uncomfortable with the situation as Lori and Robert were. He attempted to read Tommy his rights, but it was clear he did not comprehend.

Tony confided that he had already gone to the District Attorney himself requesting the charges be dropped due to the diagnosis and functioning level but he was denied. It was bigger than him and us. He was so kind to Tommy. He offered him candy and referred to him as "buddy." He told us to go by the lower floor on our way out to get Tommy some stickers. We did just that. He told us he would note in the report that Tommy was not able to understand his legal rights, which prevented him from following proper procedure.

Tommy's criminal attorneys had attempted to reason with the District Attorney several times but they both had come to the conclusion there was an agenda and Tommy was caught in the middle. Lori was told that they were aiming to set an example using Tommy. Their message was, "they will not tolerate aggression in schools." Really, she thought sarcastically? She couldn't believe it. She was all for stopping violence in schools. But, doesn't that apply to the teens who are premeditating vicious acts or crimes against teachers or fellow students. It was like she had fallen asleep one night and woke up the next morning in some weird parallel universe where right was wrong and wrong was right.

The attorneys were working hard behind the scenes and pulled some strings to arrange a private hearing with all parties in front of the presiding judge. They also arranged a private room for Tommy anytime he was required to go to the courthouse, to reduce his anxiety and exposure to potentially

129

frightening situations.

Meeting day arrived with the judge. They entered the judge's chambers and Tommy was shaking like a leaf. He has overheard people talking enough times that he has picked up on fears. He has figured out things are serious and he is scared but is not able to grasp the entire situation due to limited understanding. Lori wonders if that might not be the cruelest part of all. He is fearful but doesn't comprehend the giant he is facing. He is completely at the mercy of others.

Lori holds his hand and tells him everything will be okay. The judge calls the meeting to order and after a brief summary of the reason for the meeting, he begins to address Tommy directly. His voice is initially stern, but within minutes, he softens and looks perplexed by the innocence of the teenager in front of him. The judge realizes that Tommy is obviously special needs and terrified. His answers and confusion make it clear he does not understand what the judge is saying to him. He is trying really hard to be brave.

Lori and Robert are shocked by what the judge does next. He pulls out some Reese's cups from his giant throne and offers Tommy some candy. Tommy loves Reese's cups, so he immediately darts from his seat, before Lori can stop him, and runs up to the judge. Instead of running to the front of the Judge's bench, Tommy runs up the stairs, directly to the throne, face to face to join him in having some candy. Several people gasp, while others chuckle.

The judge smiles both at Tommy and then at Lori. It is apparent to all watching that the young man in this courtroom is someone you would expect to meet at Special Olympics, not criminal court. The judge stands up and offers his throne to Tommy. Lori seriously can't believe it. Tommy, who is oblivious to the privilege that is being given to him, dives into the judge's chair, swinging it around as he enjoys his Reece's cup. He looks like a large overgrown toddler with a contagious smile on his face. Lori's heart is full of gratitude and respect for the judge before her.

Lori and Robert look at each other but remain quite, afraid to say anything. They look across the table at legal counsel only to realize they all appear speechless. Both Tommy's attorneys and opposing counsel are witnessing a unique and unheard of event, at least in a criminal courtroom setting. Thank you, God, Lori whispers as she fights back tears watching Tommy's innocent enjoyment of candy and a fun chair, once again oblivious as to why he is here. The judge orders that Tommy be evaluated by a professional to determine if moving forward is even appropriate. The DA insists that they use their own state professional. The judge nods in agreement.

So it continues.

More evaluations, more trips to the courthouse, and more emotional stress. Tommy's attorneys warn that the state evaluator has the legal right to talk to Tommy alone and most likely will. The date is set. Great, more waiting and worrying, she thinks. The evaluation is months out. Lori and Robert have started back to church and it has helped some, but Lori is just not her outgoing self anymore. The situation is still all too heavy, looming out in the distance. She is struggling with depression. The years have taken a toll on her. She feels isolated, alone, and deeply sad. We do not fit anywhere, she thinks.

Tommy's aggressive behavior completely stopped once he was no longer attending the public school. He was compliant and completed the school work Lori gave him at home. He was less negative and really enjoyed getting together with the other home school students every other Friday. He was not isolated anymore and no one treated him unkindly. He was apologizing less and seemed to be enjoying life for the first time in a long time. He seemed relieved to be out of that toxic environment. He never talked about missing it and said he was, "happy with home school." Lori didn't blame him.

Time passes and admittedly she is starting to feel a little better. The charges were still looming but without the daily worry of school or getting a phone call, her spirits seem a little lighter. They start enjoying church and Tommy really likes the youth leader. He is outgoing and very accepting of differences. It is like day and night from his school experience. It is just what he needs. Truth be told, it is just what she and Robert need too.

Late fall ushers in evaluation day. Today is the day. The

lobby is dingy and cold. Lori is shaking from head to toe but she isn't sure if it is because she is cold or scared to death. They are sitting there in silence, feeling the stares of passer bys. It feels like everyone walking by sees them as criminals. There is no private room this time. No attorneys, just them. They are out in the open, being judged like common criminals. What a joke, she thinks, as she glances at Tommy.

The evaluator approaches them with a smile but keeps a cool, professional distance. He asks Tommy to go with him to a private office so they can talk. Tommy looks to Lori for assurance. She tells him it is okay to go with the stranger, as her hearts breaks on the inside. The man tells them it will take approximately 2 to 3 hours and they are welcome to go grab a bite to eat or wait in the lobby if they would like to.

Tommy looks back just before he turns the corner and the fear in his eyes is apparent. It is just too much. The tears streak down her face as she prays silently for her sweet son, so innocent. His aggression has never been out of meanness or violence. His ability to communicate is really limited. If he feels fearful or overwhelmed emotionally, it will bubble out in physical form. She can only imagine how he might answer the evaluator's questions. Lori just keeps praying but deep down inside, she still doubts. She still doesn't understand why God won't heal Tommy or why their lives have to be so hard. She still feels hurt and abandoned.

Even though things have been better, she has been struggling with depression on and off, which only tends to make things feel worse. What would it be like to have a "normal" life, she wonders? She longs for something in common with all the other families around her, some normalcy, but it is a dream that seems lost. The pain is deep but her love for her son is deeper. Things have been easier since we started home-school. Maybe the sun will rise and shine warmth and light into the darkness they have been walking through. She feels encouraged by the thought. If we can just get through this legal stuff, she sighs. Robert pats her hand and then wraps his arms around her as they sit and wait.

The evaluator traveled here from several hours away, her

132

mind continuing to fire off thoughts. He is unaware of any agenda. Does he know anything about autism, she wonders? What if he says Tommy is competent to stand trial? Surely not, she consoles herself. However, these past two years have taught her to expect the unexpected. The thought sends panic throughout her body. Her mind is a teeter-totter of thoughts and emotions, some up and some down. Where will they land when the teetering stops...?

The depression phase of A-typical Cyclic Grief is a very typical response to the challenges and emotional waves experienced within the journey. You may have experienced it briefly or have cycled in and out of it. Hopefully, like Lori, it ebbs and flows with the ups and downs. For others, it may occur more frequently.

Not all parents that experience A-typical Cyclic Grief will have the same level of demands or restrictions placed on their lives. However, the loss of "normal" and the emotional cycles around that loss is universally experienced by all of us. You can certainly understand why Lori is struggling with some depression. She is overwhelmed by the situations they are facing, on top of living with the daily loss of "normal" and the challenges posed by the disability or limitations.

I am not going to spend time on the clinical aspects of depression because there is a sea of books on the subject, including signs, symptoms, and treatment. However, learning to work through the emotional cycles that come with A-typical Cyclic Grief may help you get through the temporary waves of situational depression created by the loss of "normal" more effectively. The depression described in ACG is referring to situational type depression.

In situational depression, the sadness usually lessens once the situation improves or enough time passes since the situation has occurred. A clear life example of this would be if someone loses their job, they may experience a time of depression related to that loss. Eventually, when they find another job, that depression will subside because the situation has changed or improved. The depression is attached to that specific loss, and in time, will decrease either because the situation has changed or they have adapted to the change.

You should expect that you will have times throughout your life, as you watch your child experience the loss of "normal", and you experience the loss of "normal", where you will feel sad and isolated. It is a loss.

If the depression you experience is sustained over time and does not get better or it interferes with your ability to go about your daily life, seek out a professional for assessment and help to deal with the depression. If you have any thoughts of harming yourself such as suicidal thoughts, you need to seek help immediately. The National Suicide Prevention Lifeline is 1-800-273-TALK or suicidepreventionlifeline.org. Depression is not to be taken lightly, nor am I suggesting we just brush it off.

I am suggesting we will experience times of feeling isolated and sadness/depression in a cyclic nature as we experience ACG. Talking with friends or getting into a support group with others that can relate to your situation reduces feelings of isolation and can really relieve symptoms of depression.

When we feel understood, connected, and hopeful, situational depression tends to let up. Find ways to reach out and get out of the house. Even internet forums with other parents that have children with like disabilities can make you feel more connected. Take time for yourself. Do something you enjoy that can give you a mental vacation from all the troubles. Exercises, art, meditation, yoga, music, hiking, are just a few examples of ways we can refuel our mind, heart, and body.

Proper care of ourselves and our own needs is going to be an important aspect of healthy parenting. Our parenting may need to last much longer than typical parents are required to remain on the job. I understand that once you are a parent you are forever a parent. But kids that do not have a developmental disability typically do not live with parents indefinitely. Our health, both mentally and physically, needs to be given proper attention.

If you have ever flown on an airplane, then you know that when they give the life- saving instructions, they always tell you to place the oxygen mask on yourself before trying to help others, especially your children. Why? It is simple really. An unconscious parent can't help their child. The same principle exists here. You have to take care of yourself to be able to properly take care of your child. Answer the following questions as you begin to think about depressions you may have faced.

Challenge Questions:

1. **Have you experienced or are you experiencing feelings of depression?**

2. **What situation(s) are increasing your feelings of depression?**

3. **Have you talked with anyone about your feelings?**

4. **Is the depression affecting your ability to go about your everyday life?**

5. **When was the last time you did something to take care of yourself?**

6. **Make a list of at least 5 things you would love to do that would make you feel refreshed or reenergized. Think about things like a bubble bath, a massage, a night out with friends etc.**

7. **Plan a time that you will do each of the things on your list.**

Remember: You have to put your oxygen mask on first to be able to care for your child!

Chapter 13: Back in the Saddle.

Every tick of the second hand feels like an hour. It's brutal. The cold impersonal lobby seems to accuse the people waiting within its walls, regardless of guilt or innocence. Twenty minutes of torture, wondering, waiting, and praying for Tommy, and so far it feels like an eternity. What if he tells this evaluator he understands his rights? What if this evaluator only asks him yes or no questions? He almost always answers yes whether he understands the question or not. Her thoughts are a swirling pool of fear. Suddenly, she sees Tommy round the corner.

The evaluator is joking with him about a sports team and telling him what a good job he did. He tells Tommy to wait with his dad and asks Lori if she will come back to talk with him. Lori is not sure what to make of the situation because she had been told prior, even by the evaluator, that Tommy would be with him for at least two hours. It has only been 20 minutes. She wasn't able to decide if this was good or bad, and she is teetering on sheer panic.

As soon as the door closes and they sit down, the evaluator asks Lori to tell him what is really going on. She is taken back by his question. What do you mean? , she asks in response to the question. "I've been doing this job for many years, and I know when something is off. What is the agenda here, he asks?" Before she could answer, he went on. "Is it school? Are they trying to force him out because his behavior is too challenging?" Lori wasn't sure, but she thought she perceived irritation, almost offense in his voice. He told her he had read the reports and after speaking with Tommy, he did not see anything that justified the criminal charges against him.

Lori felt relief wash over her. It was like someone had lifted a thousand pound weight off her shoulders. The evaluator explained; Tommy's behavior is consistent with his diagnosis and should have never resulted in charges. He also said charges were inappropriate based on his level of understanding. He told Lori it was clear within the first five minutes that he was not competent to stand trial, but Tommy was so worried about doing a good job that he spent extra time with him allowing him to answer simple questions and telling him what a great job he was doing. Lori was amazed by his compassion and caring for Tommy.

This man, who had never met Tommy before, went on to tell her that it is easy to see that he is eager to please and wants to do the right thing. Lori decided to trust the man and tell him the truth about her suspicions. She told him about Ms. Ford and everything that had occurred over the past two years. He listened carefully. She told him about her fear of sending Tommy back to school. She also talked about how much better Tommy is doing since he no longer has to be in isolation.

The evaluator told Lori that the school system has an obligation to educate Tommy. He also told her she has the right to not live in fear of further charges if he does have a meltdown at school. He asks her to consider putting him back in the school system, because he is going to write a report that would make it impossible for any future charges to stick or even be filed in the first place.

It is clear to her that this man is outraged by the actions of the school system, and the District Attorney's decision to move forward with charges. He tells her he is going to make it known to the DA that these charges are inappropriate and highlight a serious lack of due diligence as well as professionalism within that office. The venom is audible as he speaks. Lori fights the urge to stand up and cheer. Finally, someone with a brain and a heart speaking the truth; the irony, it's the D.A.'s own state evaluator they pushed the judge to allow. Tommy's attorneys had requested an evaluator that specializes in autism. The judge ruled in favor of the state evaluator. Maybe the judge knew this would be the outcome, Lori thought.

The evaluator is an encouraging, kind man, by her assessment. He says he understands if she decides to keep Tommy in home-school for his own well- being. He also commends her for advocating for her son and apologizes on the behalf of the entire legal system for what she, Tommy, and Robert have had to endure. It wasn't his place to apologize but his apologies warm her heart.

She turned the corner to see Robert sitting with Tommy, laughing and joking with him, keeping his mood light and fears at

137

bay. Her heart fills at the sight. My Robert, what would we do without you? , she thinks. She hopes she never has to find out. They walked out of that dingy, cold lobby with the accusatory walls, never to return after that day. Feeling lighter than she has in years, Lori smiles as she walks away. For the first time in a long time, she feels a sliver of hope for the future.

She and Robert decide to keep Tommy in home-school for his own mental health and happiness. Ultimately, they decide that Tommy's emotional well-being is more important than winning a battle with the school system.

Several years later, with the charges in their past, Lori is delighted that things have continued to go well. All charges were dismissed and the horror of those final years in the school system is behind them. Tommy really enjoys the outings with his school friends and is very proud to be a senior this year. It does not escape her that he has not had one meltdown or behavioral outburst since leaving the school system.

Sometimes she wonders about all the reasons he has been outburst free, but she settles for just being grateful the rough years are over. She looks outside and realizes it is starting to sprinkle rain. Perfect, she thinks sarcastically. I have to get these decorations to the gym to prepare for prom and this is all we need, wet decorations, ugh. It is May and his senior prom is tomorrow. He has picked out a suit and is looking forward to the occasion.

Tommy has completed an entire year of internship through a special needs program in the community this year. He worked at a golf course, maintaining the carts and keeping up the grounds, alongside others of course. He was proud of his job; it seemed to give him a sense of belonging, and a sense of purpose.

Lori is a little nervous about prom. She knows how much he is looking forward to the event and wants him to have his cherished moment, just like every parent wants for their teen. Lord knows he deserves it, she thinks.

The clock strikes six. He looks very handsome, strutting around in his suit, anxiously awaiting the moment to leave. Lori insists on pictures, of course. Doesn't every mom want pictures, she thinks. She tells Tommy to smile and again it looks more like he is gritting his teeth than posing for the camera. It makes her smile. Robert decides to tickle him, hoping to create a few natural grins as she snaps away trying to capture the moment. She and Robert are helping with the prom and Tommy is happy to have them along.

Most teens would be mortified to have their parents at their prom, she thinks. Not Tommy. If there is an upside to his innocence, it may be that he enjoys his parents coming along. We are his companions, she acknowledges honestly. They all pile into Tommy's truck, which he got for graduation.

He is learning to drive. Well actually, he has been learning to drive for three years, she muses. He is a very safe driver and follows all the rules; exactly follows the rules. He only likes to drive on roads with very little traffic, so it limits his practice, but in time, she believes he will be able to get his license and perhaps make small trips independently. Tommy is grinning from ear to ear as they drive the twenty minutes to his home-school gym.

Lori admits, as they walk in, the place looks great. The decorations are perfect and it looks just like every other high school prom she has seen. She is so glad they decided to keep Tommy in this home-school program. The directors have even made him a special diploma that looks just like all the other kids. He is not graduating with a standard diploma. He is not academically able to complete high school work. He can do a lot of other things though, Lori thinks.

In fact, she starts pouring over the past couple of years where things have really become quite easy. He still struggles here and there, but he is on the right track. Maybe he will get a job one day, she hopes. She feels like she has finally figured out how to live a life that is not what she expected it would be. Yes, he has limitations, but at least she knows what they are and how to manage them. They pushed through all those hard times and now they are back in the saddle of life. Making progress, hope for many tomorrows.

She hears the music fire up. Tommy takes his seat at the Senior's table. She and Robert sit with the other volunteers. He looks so happy. She knows he will not eat any of the food being served but that's not a problem. She anticipated this, so he ate before he came.

The kids are nice to him and finally talk him into getting on the dance floor. The sight is such a thrill to watch. Tommy having fun with peers is not something she thought would happen a few years ago. They are not friends in the way that most people would define friendship, Lori acknowledges. They don't invite him to hang out with them or do teenage things. But, they are kind to him here at school and that definitely counts for something.

The announcement ceremony of Mr. and Ms. SGH court begins; Lori is half listening and half watching her son out of the corner of her eye. She knows Tommy will not be on the court, so her attention easily drifts back to the senior table to watch the interactions of his classmates while the director is talking. The queen's crown is brought out on an ornate pillow and the king will be given a gold medallion. Tommy is watching but it is not keeping his attention either. He looks bored and ready to get back out on the dance floor. That's okay, she thinks, at least he is here.

The director is talking about how the candidates are selected by student vote. She first announces the runners up in the female category. Next, she starts describing the character of this year's queen. The anticipation is building among the senior girls. The director engages in a long pause before announcing the Ms. SGH. Without further ado, this year's queen is Sandy Ellis. No surprise there, Lori muses. She is a beautiful girl both inside and out. Excellent choice, Lori thinks. She notices the disappointment on a few of the other girl's faces as they try to cover it up with a huge smile and congratulations for their friend.

The male category is coming up and she is guessing who she thinks will be prom king based on her knowledge of these kids. She has been a parent volunteer and has come to know them fairly well. Again, the director pauses, but this time she seems to be composing herself emotionally. She says to the crowd in a shaky voice, "This year our king was chosen slightly differently." Lori perks up. She goes on. "I was approached by several of our seniors, both male and female, who told me they

140

all voted on one prom king to represent Mr. SGH and they did not want any runner-ups." "It was unanimous. They explained to me how and why they came to their decision, so I agreed." The look shared by lower classmen and chaperones made it clear everyone was now curious.

She began to describe the character of the young man they all voted as Mr. SGH. His fellow classmates describe him as honest, kind to everyone, a hard worker, funny, and always eager to help. His classmates believe he provides an example for all of us to follow. Lori's mind is desperately trying to figure out who it is. She thinks she has it narrowed down to two possibilities.

The director opens the envelope and announces with great pride, "Our prom king and Mr. SGH this year is Tommy Jones." The place erupts with applause. Lori is overcome with emotions and begins to cry as she watches Tommy walk up on the stage with the help of his classmates. She just can't believe it! Tommy was definitely not one of the two she had in mind. The applause grows louder as he takes his place on stage. He is smiling as the director bestows the medallion around his neck to honor him as Mr. SGH. Lori jumps to her feet to take pictures of her smiling teenage son being honored by his classmates. The sight continues to bring her to tears. She snaps away through the fog of her own tears.

Lori wasn't sure who looked more proud. They were all beaming. Tommy, the director, and his classmates, who worked behind the scenes to make this happen, was bursting with pride. It was beautiful. What a turnaround from the years of isolation when he wasn't even allowed to eat with his classmates, Lori thinks. Is this what it is like to experience the typical joys of parenthood, she wonders? She knew deep down that Tommy was not chosen for the usual reasons, but it still felt wonderful to watch Tommy have his moment in the sun. It felt wonderful to watch the kindness of others sow joy in his life.

Graduation was equally fantastic. He looked striking in his cap and gown. All of Robert and Lori's family came to celebrate his graduation. It finally felt like he was a part of life in some small way, instead of on the fringes. He was finally not that different from everyone else. He still has some limitations but who knows in time what he might achieve. The last two years have been fairly good. "normal" felt closer than it has in a long time. She feels like she and Tommy have come ashore from an epic sea journey. Finally, they have gained their footing on dry ground. Hope is alive and Lori is ready to ride this tide that brought them ashore from here on out....

You can sense Lori's rejuvenated confidence and hope. Maybe you are thinking, it's about time because they have been through the ringer. Or maybe you are wishing you could find hope and confidence again. If you haven't yet, you will experience this emotional phase of renewed hope along your journey. Oftentimes, it occurs when developmental advancements are on a steady climb. If your child is really making great progress, it will give you hope that he or she may catch up or at least continue to grow at a good rate.

If your child's behavior improves, which makes it easier for you to do things in the community such as shopping, church, or going out to eat, your life will feel more "normal" and you will have greater hope for the future. That's really what Lori is experiencing. Basically, when we and our children are able to do many of the things that other people enjoy without additional challenges, it lessens our grief. We feel more connected to our society, more "normal."

Sounds simple right? Maybe it is, but it also sets us up in ways we may not expect. When we are processing through A-typical Cyclic Grief (ACG), we may come to accept that our child has a disability and know that our lives will forevermore be changed early on in the grief process. However, as we cycle through trying to figure out what we are up against, the situation is constantly changing.

Our children will grow and change through the years, so we have no idea what they will be able to achieve or not. We can only adjust to where they are in the moment or where we hope they will be based on what they can do in the here and now. So, if things are great, we expect they will stay great and our child or children will have a shot at a "normal" or semi-"normal" life. If things are really challenging, we begin to lose hope or feel fearful about the future.

Our grief, in many ways, is directly attached to our child's progress or hope of progress. The diagnosis only represents the initial awareness that life will not be as expected. The functioning and progress of the child defines the depth of that loss. As we and our children go through life, their present level of functioning psychologically resets our new life script.

Lori's renewed sense of hope is based on Tommy's present level of functioning. Hope is good, and I'm thankful that we as parents experience times that our kid's progress gives us a renewed hope. Hope is not the problem. The problem is hope coming and going with each new change in functioning levels. It creates cycles or waves of new grief.

Sometimes, just when you think you have it figured out, it changes again. You might be thinking, well that's just life. Yes, that's true. Life does constantly change, but what I'm talking about is different. Children and adults without a developmental disability will change, certainly, but overall some things are expected. Things like talking, walking, eating, potty training, reading, writing, socializing, dating, driving, graduation, work, and basic independence will be expected, for starters. It is unknown for many of our children whether they will achieve those expected norms or not.

The ups and downs in their abilities cause us to continuously rewrite the script. Remember, we don't have the "normal" psychological script to follow anymore. We are in uncharted waters.

It is natural to fear the unknown and resist change, for some more than others. We all crave predictability; it is human nature. One of the most challenging aspects of A-typical Cyclic Grief is the constant changes we face as parents. Hope is important and we need to find hope no matter where our child is functioning. Whether the highest or lowest functioning ability, I believe we can adapt and find hope wherever our circumstances place us.

If you are walking this road less traveled with me, then you know the powerful love and inspirations our children bring far outweigh the grief, many times, along the way. The renewed sense of hope stage is where we experience confidence in our ability to manage the challenges while still enjoying the positive aspects of life.

Lori is in the "I've got this stage." However, her confidence may cause her to be blindsided by future setbacks or losses such as unmet milestones. Just like Lori, this phase can give us parents a false sense of "normal". As we continue in the book, we will learn how to arrive at a healthy place of "I've got this." We will learn how to change our perspectives and redefine normal. Take a few moments to work through the following questions.

Challenge Questions:

1. Have you experienced or are you currently experiencing a renewed sense of hope stage?

2. What is or was happening in your child's life during that time?

3. Can you remember a time that you felt hopeless? What is or was going on in your child's life that made you feel that way?

4. If you think about how your vision for your child's future or your own future changed between the hopeful and hopeless phases, were they different? In what ways?

5. Are you currently or have you struggled in the past to nail down your expectations?

6. What hopes and dreams do you have for your child or adult child?

7. Are those hopes or dreams tied to societal norms such as living independently, socializing, holding down a job, having friends, driving, dating, etc?

8. What hopes do you have for your child that is not tied to societal norms? Like Happiness? Self-worth? Etc.

Remember: Hope is powerful but hope that is only awakened by achievement is NOT a trustworthy hope.

Chapter 14: I Didn't See that Coming!

They all arrive around the same time. She watches James park his truck, climb out, and run to the other side to open the door for his girlfriend Pam. At least he learned some things from his father, Lori thinks. Carrie is walking toward them, luggage in tow, talking about how wonderful the warm ocean breeze feels. She is a high-level executive living in the north, climbing the ladder of success. She hugs Tommy and her daddy before walking around the car to hug Lori.

Scott and Ella had arrived the day before to finalize some last minute preparations for the wedding. Lori is ready to check into the hotel and get settled before dinner. She suggests they all go out to eat as a family tonight. Everyone is in favor of the idea, so the plans are set. Tommy reaches out to hug James and Pam. They both return his hug with warmth.

Tommy is constantly asking about James and Pam, especially if James will take him to the movies. The memory causes Lori to feel annoyed. Tommy is lonely most of the time because he doesn't have any same age friends. James was the closest thing he had to a peer buddy growing up. James was nice to Tommy but didn't ever initiate spending time with him on his own, except for one rare occasion. He was never really interested in having a relationship with Tommy. However, Tommy adored him.

For that matter, none of us have seen James very much since he started driving, including Robert. Deep down it pains her to see James, the son that is so close in age to Tommy, surpass Tommy in every way. The pain is even more acute, when James is dismissive of Tommy. Some things never change, she thinks irritably with sadness in her heart.

It has been a long time since they have all been together and she is weary of how the night will unfold. By 7:00 p.m., they all meet back in the parking lot to go out for dinner. Tommy wants to ride with James, but he says his truck is too full. It may be true, but Tommy is visibly dejected nonetheless. Carrie pipes up and asks Tommy if he would like to ride with her. She watches James pull behind them as they head towards the restaurant; old feelings of resentment are creeping back up. It *tends to happen often around James, mostly because of how he treats Tommy, she admits.*

    The restaurant is busy, but they still manage to get a table to accommodate them all in just fewer than thirty minutes. The night goes fairly well, everyone catching up and sharing stories. Tommy sits beside Lori, occasionally joining the conversations when she draws him in. This is much harder than she thought it would be, Lori realizes. Seeing James with his girlfriend so grown up; driving, dating, and still dismissive towards Tommy, makes her want to ignore him just to prove a point. Now, now, she chides herself. Don't be ridiculous. He just doesn't get it, she thinks.

    She and James have never been close. After all this time, it is hard to sort out the why. She has tried over the years; James was not receptive even as a young child to a close relationship. He kept a good distance from her and Tommy. They had some fond memories together, none that were terrible, but not enough fond memories to build a meaningful relationship. Lori has built a decent relationship with both Scott and Carrie throughout the years and it still saddens her to this day that she can't say the same for James.

    Robert has been a dedicated father to James, never missing a game and always understanding if James had something he would rather do than see his father. All sitting together at the table, Lori glances over her shoulder at Tommy. The togetherness makes her wonder what he would be like without autism. What would his girlfriend be like, what would be his interests, his favorite topic of conversation? Stop it! , she screams in her head. She realizes everyone is done eating and conversation is starting to wane. She suggests they all call it a night so they can be rested for the big day tomorrow.

    It had been a picture perfect day, Lori thinks. The sound of the waves crashing on the shore and the seagulls singing in the air above her emphasizes the beauty of the white sand beneath her feet and breathtaking sunset. The sun setting over open water gives the illusion that you can actually see the world curve out of sight; if it were flat you might see the other side. Lori smiles as she tries to distract herself from the wedding in front of

147

her. Something is gnawing at her on the inside.

Robert looks so amazingly handsome in his wedding attire. He is so proud, father of the groom. Scott and Ella have been dating for a couple of years and today they make it official. Scott, Robert's oldest son, has matured quite a bit and settled on a career and family life. He is handsome, just like Robert, and Ella is breathtakingly beautiful. Scott asked both James and Tommy to be groomsman for the wedding. Lori has to admit, James who is months away from leaving for college, has grown into a handsome young man with a promising academic future. She is proud of him and does love him, despite her own emotional struggles with him and Tommy.

The service is well underway when it hits. The sight before her cuts like a knife. Lori is struck by deep anguish. She feels a pain so deep it takes her breath away. It hits her like a Mack truck out of nowhere. What is happening? , she thinks. She is blindsided by the emotions.

She is so happy for Scott and Ella; she has come to love both of them dearly. But this is not about them. This is grief! She knows it all too well. Her heart is pounding and her stomach is doing somersaults, end over end. She is weighed down by the anxiety that feels like a panic attack. Seeing Tommy side by side in a line up with his brothers and sister, the contrast of everything he will never be, never have, is heart wrenching. It's like someone dangling a carrot in front of her, saying this is for everyone else. Not only will you never taste it, but you will have to watch everyone else enjoy it, while you are left with nothing but the loss of what should have been. Her heart feels shattered into a million pieces.

She feels so guilty that she is overcome with grief at Scott's wedding. She has been battling negative feelings but has managed to keep them suppressed, clinging to the belief that it is just old feelings. These are not old feelings, she admits. This is a fresh new wave of loss.

Tommy has been doing so well and somehow in their little corner of life it has felt pretty normal. She was not prepared for this living portrait, cruelly highlighting the sum of all of Tommy's losses, her losses. She looks up to see Scott saying his vows and the love she sees the two of them share. Momentarily, she feels such joy for them. But the aching hurt in the pit of her gut overrules the joy.

The realization that Tommy is alone is not new. None of this is new; she is confused by this onslaught of grief. It feels like she has been walking on the red carpet of life, hitting a nice stride, then suddenly she trips on some invisible wrinkle, knocking the breath out of her, leaving her lying face down on the floor. This is so unfair! Why? Why Tommy, she questions? Why my little boy? Why does he have to suffer so many losses?

It felt like she was being crushed by the ocean waves she can hear crashing against the shore in the background. It was as if each wave was jeering at her with each blow; no wedding for him, no love for him, no college for him, no family for him, no children for him, no grandchildren for him, no career for him, no friends for him, and so on, the jeering continues. Will this grief ever end? She feels angry and resentful. She is angry at God, angry at autism, but mostly, she is angry at herself for her own thoughts. Why is she feeling this way? She knows he has autism. She knows! She feels ashamed of her thoughts and negativity but the hurt remains. She loves Tommy so much; she tries to suck it up and wills herself to focus on the positive.

The tears running down her cheeks are a reflection of mixed emotions. They are tears of joy for Scott and his beautiful wife Ella, tears of joy for Robert, and tears of deep sorrow for Tommy and for her. Sorrow for the life she expected her son to have, the life Tommy deserves, and the losses they must face at every turn. She doesn't pray. She doesn't know what to say to God any more when it comes to Tommy.

She is thankful for so many things, honestly. But the healing she has asked for has not been granted and she has been asking for well over 10 years. She wants the hurt to stop. She wants Tommy to have what everyone else gets to enjoy. She wants him to have a "normal" life with love, friendship, and independence. Maybe God doesn't want to heal Tommy or maybe she isn't worthy. The thought crushes her and makes her feel all the more abandoned by God.

She looks around at the world and wonders why people

who don't even believe or care about God seem to have these wonderful lives. It feels so unfair, so unjust. She feels somewhat resentful that she has served God and believed for so many years, yet she and her son have to endure such hardships while God allows it to happen. It hardly seems right.

She can remember having such faith when she was younger, but now she feels mostly disappointment. She just wants God to make things better. Is that too much to ask, she wonders? The bitterness that is growing inside scares her.

On the way home from the wedding, she is reflecting on the events of the past week. The wedding was truly beautiful! The reception was equally fun. She is so grateful that Ella is very inclusive and thoughtful. Ella had included her in part of the planning, just as if she had been mother-in-law by birthright. She never treated Lori like she was the stepmother-in-law. Scott and Ella were both kind to Tommy but struggled to understand how to fully relate to him. We all struggle to relate to him at times, Lori thought.

Tommy did well in his role as groomsman. He was only distracted a few times. He has learned how to control the echolalia (the self talk he does when he is over-stimulated) through the years. He can hold it in until he gets alone, and then he lets it all out at one time, she muses. He is aware of people's stares, and sometimes Lori wonders what all he is aware of but not able to communicate. The thought is frightening to her. Does he feel alone? He has cried before because he did not have any friends and felt left out, she recalls. Does he want a girlfriend? Does he want someone to spend his life with and love? Does he feel trapped by the autism? That would be horrible, she shutters at the thought.

The wedding was a mixed bag all together, she decides. She was so thankful that she got along well with Ella's family. Roberts's ex-wife was not an easy person to get along with, so it made family gatherings difficult at times. Lori was happy to be headed home, back to their little corner of life, the corner that keeps their losses hidden in the shadows of their reality. Even though she wasn't sure she would be able to shake this new heaviness, the thoughts of being more isolated are comforting.

She feels frustrated that no one told her what to expect. No one warned her that she would have grief on and off for the rest of her life. No one told her she would have grief at all and that it was normal! She is almost angry. Maybe if I would have known I could have prepared, she thinks.

She is angry because a joyous celebration was overshadowed by emptiness, because it was another reminder of what Tommy will never have, of what she will never have. Maybe if she would have had other children, typical children, the loss would not be as bad. Tommy is her only child. She isn't sure, but she guesses the grief would still be there no matter how many children you bore.

As she is staring out the window, she is thinking about the hidden nature of her grief. Grieving in silence is hard. She doesn't want to take away from Robert's joy and would feel guilty admitting her feelings to him. She literally feels like she has just learned of the diagnosis all over again, but this time she can't talk about it, not to anyone. The silence is deafening.

How did she not see this coming? Has she been in denial? Is every joyous event going to be a source of pain? Deep down she almost resents Robert because he has what she doesn't. He is able to experience his son's wedding. He is able to anticipate becoming a grandfather. He gets the privilege of watching his child fall in love and that love being returned, while she watches her child flounder, alone. She feels completely alone, despite the fact that Robert is sitting next to her, holding her hand as they travel home. No one understands this hurt. How could they, she whispers under her breath? Tears sting her eyes. They arrive back home and throw themselves back into life. In time, she feels better as the safety net of their sheltered existence insulates her from the outside world.

It has been almost a year since Scott's wedding. Spring rolls around flaunting its display of beautiful wild flowers and warm sunny days. Lori feels pretty good although she never fully recovered from the wedding. The losses she had to face that day never left her mind.

They are attending church regularly and Tommy loves his youth group. There are some really sweet kids and his youth *leader is exceptional at including everyone, even Tommy. He is a Cajun man with a heart of gold. Tommy wants to go on a youth trip this summer and Lori is dreading it. She wants him to go, but the thoughts of watching him with other kids day after day, for five days, is like going on a vacation through an emotional safari. They sign up to go nonetheless, she as a chaperone and Tommy as a youth.*

What if he starts to have a meltdown? What if the kids ignore him? What if he is disruptive in the service? What if, what if, what if, never stops; the anxiety is in full bloom. Summer rolls around and the bus pulls out at 6:00 a.m. with sixty youth aboard; Lori is weighed down by a strong sense of impending doom…

Lori's experience at the wedding is a firsthand peek at how grief can reset when we are faced with a milestone that our child or children will never reach. She was doing so well with her renewed sense of hope and really believed she was done with the grieving process because she had accepted Tommy's disability. She had! But, accepting Tommy has a disability is different from understanding that she will continue to grieve when future milestones are not met. Understanding the nature of our grief and the longevity of our grief doesn't happen magically when we accept our child has a disability.

Think about it. When our children are young, we are not trying to teach them how to get married or have children, at least I hope not. We are focusing on helping them be successful in school, making friends, basic living skills, etc. We are hopeful that all of our efforts and theirs will pay off one day. We do not psychologically prepare for futuristic missed milestones. One reason may be we are too busy and overwhelmed just trying to focus on the here and now. The other is simply the, "You don't know what you don't know," lack of awareness.

The cyclic nature of our grief is unique. If your child is doing very well, you have a renewed sense of hope for "normal" or close to "normal", but if or when he/she regresses or hits a wall, you may experience the grief cycle all over again. Sometimes those walls are unmet milestones.

It creates a yoyo effect. You can see the ebb and flow in Lori's life. She has moved in and out of hope as Tommy moves closer to "normal" and farther away from "normal". Grief can feel like a yoyo moving up and down on the string of life. It can feel like we are stuck on a treadmill, never reaching a destination but always running at full speed.

I don't know about you, but I don't want to be stuck on an emotional treadmill the rest of my life. Let me be clear. We will still experience grief throughout our child's lifespan, especially surrounding unmet milestones. However, the ebb and flow of our children's progress does not have to dictate our hope. I remember my first unmet milestone experience. It completely caught me off guard and sent me spiraling emotionally.

It was February 16th and we were celebrating our son's 16th birthday! Wow! I couldn't believe he was sixteen years old. He was diagnosed at four years old, so we had been adjusting to his diagnosis for twelve years. Those years were full of joys, tears, challenges, and most of all interventions, to give him every opportunity to be an independent adult. It's funny how when he was young, it seemed like adulthood was so far away and potentially held so much promise. It was like in the future we would meet an older, higher functioning version of this child we were teaching. He might go to college, drive, date, who knows.

By the time he was sixteen, I thought I had a handle on this grief thing. I was accepting of his limitations and the emotional struggle was behind me. Boy was I wrong! I had not anticipated how I would feel when 16 hit.

It is the year that marks driving, a child's first car, independence, and maybe even a part time job. As I dropped him off at school and looked around at all the kids he had grown up with, it was like a kick in the gut all over again. The grief and loss was unbearable. It was like I was realizing again for the first time that he was living in a world that was leaving him behind.

All the little kids that encircled him in elementary school were now encircling each other at bonfires, parties, dates, and school functions, none of which he was included in. They were all still kind to him, but the undeniable truth was, he was not part of their world. He was living life outside of "normal" and it ripped my heart out.

I was devastated and completely unprepared for this new wave of emotions. I questioned my response. How could I be experiencing grief at this level when I have lived with his disability for so many years? Just a few months ago things seemed fine.

I had come face to face with my first monumental unmet milestone! The focus up until that point had been school, friends, social skills, and behavior. I had not mentally prepared for the changing milestones that lay just ahead and the deep loss I would feel as I watched him left behind once again.

That loss still causes a deep pain in my soul, even as I write these words. I grieved for all the things he would miss. His first kiss, girlfriends, dating, breakups, football games, and most of all, a sense of belonging were all out of reach. I do not believe it is entirely possible for someone to know this type of grief unless you have lived it. It is so far reaching and complex that it can literally knock the breath out of you at times.

I remember looking at my handsome son and wondering what he feels. I know he feels loss at times, because he has expressed feelings of loneliness and sadness because he does not have friends. However, his limitations made it difficult, if not impossible, for him to form friendships with his non-disabled peers. It still does to this day.

He was not in the resource room in school, so he did not have exposure or time with disabled peers that he may have been able to form friendships with. In hindsight, inclusion may have not been the best options for him, but we can only act on the information we have at the time. I did what I thought was best for him.

Watching him cry because he so desperately wanted to belong but just did not know how caused deep pain and sorrow for me as a parent. He had not caught up. All the years of interventions, which stole my total attention and focus, did not give him "normal". An emotional traffic accident with sustainable injuries had occurred at the intersection of "normal" and NOT, for both me and my son.

If you take another look at the model, you see that the unmet milestone stage is where we can either cycle back through the grief over and over again expecting different results or move out of the loop into a place of adapting to the losses, both known and future. You probably have already cycled through all of the stages at some point, so learning to break the unending cycle will lead you to adapting.

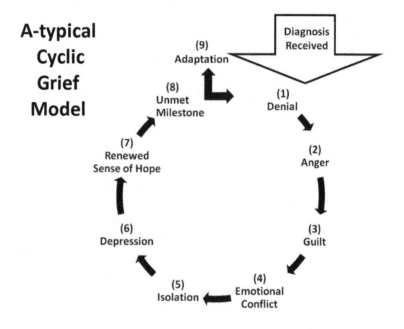

After cycling through the stages countless times myself, I am working on moving out of the cycle by adapting to our norms. We have to experience a shift in our perspective to move into the adapting phase. It means coming to terms with the losses, letting go of "normal", while also finding joy in day to day life. I am now well aware of future unmet milestones just around the corner. This awareness gives me the opportunity to process it and work through some of my emotions in advance. Instead of expecting a different outcome or chasing after "normal", I can anticipate what would be realistic for us. Somehow for me, this lessens the sting or shock that comes with unexpected grief. Maybe it will for you also.

Remember how Lori describes unmet milestones like the wrinkle in the carpet. You have hit a nice stride and are flowing with confidence when your foot hits the wrinkle and you find yourself lying face down, shell-shocked and deflated, wondering what just happened!! If we know the wrinkle is there, we can watch for it. Maybe we will stumble but not fall flat on our face.

Take some time to work through the challenge questions.

Challenge Questions:

1. **Have you faced an unmet milestone yet?**

2. **What was your experience like?**

3. **Did you see it coming?**

4. **What potential unmet milestones do you imagine in the future?**

Remember: Preparing psychologically for potential unmet milestones will not eliminate the grief but it will help you get through it without feeling blindsided.

Chapter 15: No More Chasing "Normal"! Getting Off this Treadmill.

After a six hour bus ride with 60 teenagers, Lori was either going to fling herself off at the next stop or try to medicate herself into a stupor. Luckily, she didn't have to do either. The bus pulled into the hotel parking lot just in the nick of time. The bus smelled more like a locker room with backed up commodes. The bathroom on the bus was clogged up, and the smell had been floating in the air for at least the last hour or so.

Tommy was like a kid in a candy store. He had been rotating seats, sitting by several of the teens, feeling very independent and part of the group. Lori was fighting very hard to focus on the positive. She was trying to ignore the vast developmental differences between Tommy and the other kids. They were nice to him, but he didn't have the same interactions they had with each other. It would have been impossible to ignore that obvious fact.

The youth event was a conference that hosted several Christian bands and guest speakers. It was an all weekend event with scheduled meeting times for the conference and some free time in between. The first night was really good. Actually, Lori was surprised. The speaker was good and the music was fantastic. Tommy didn't understand the speaker. The message was way over his head and the volume of the music was rock concert loud, a bit challenging for someone with autism and sensitive hearing. He didn't complain.

The next day the group did several activities together that Tommy really enjoyed. It was so nice to see him having fun. She was watching Tommy swim as she reflected on the speaker's message.

He had talked about how good God is and the gifts he gives to his children. The message was aimed at teenagers, as all of the messages will be, so she has been told. The preacher used stories that teens could relate to and did a good job keeping their attention. She was required to discuss the message with the girls in her room before bed, as part of her responsibilities as a chaperone. Lori feels a bit like a fraud, because deep down, she knows she is still angry at God and feels disappointed he hasn't lived up to his end of the bargain.

She's been praying for him to heal Tommy completely, or at least give him the ability to build friendships and hold down a job. She started praying when he was just three years old, prior to the diagnosis, she recalls. She is glad to be back in church but it also forces her to face what is deep inside, what she would rather keep buried. She doesn't have any answers and still lives with the pain in silence. Her life and Tommy's is the sum total of unmet expectations. Why? The question will never be answered. It just isn't fair.

Two hours later, they are on the bus headed to the next event. The line is super long, so it takes them at least an hour to get in and seated. The introductions begin and the event is kicked off with music. It is beautiful and upbeat. There are approximately 12,000 youth in attendance at least that is what they announced earlier. A man comes on stage and begins talking about his journey with God and declares he is a fourth generation preacher. Lori realizes she desperately needs to use the ladies room and now is her opportunity. Tommy is settled and she can slip out quietly. That is what she does.

She is a few feet away from the exit as she hears the man say, "I was asked to come here tonight to speak to teenagers, but that is not what God has told me to do." Her ears perk up! What? Why? she wonders. She stops to listen, curiosity getting the best of her. "God has put on my heart that there is an adult here tonight that has been praying for a healing for well over ten years and the healing hasn't come" the man goes on to say. Now, Lori's heart starts pounding. What is happening, she questions? Why do I feel this way?

He continues, "This person, and you know who you are, feels abandoned by God and feels distant from Him." Lori instantly feels like a spotlight is shining on her. It's as if God is speaking directly to her through this man. It is the most eerie, uncanny experience she has ever had. The man begins to tell about his father that had been diagnosed with cancer. He said they prayed for his healing, even believed it would happen.

For two years they prayed, but still he died. He admits that his faith was shattered! Everything he had ever been taught came into question. Lori realizes she has a lot in common with this preacher. Boy, can I relate, she thinks. He goes on, "God wants me to share with this person who has prayed for well over 10 years what He showed me in my time of grief." Lori is hanging on every word at this point. She doesn't know how, but this man is talking directly to her. She just knows it. She feels it. He said that God asked him a question. The question was, "When did the cross stop being enough for you?" Huh, she thinks.

The man went on to say, "God never promised us perfection or wellness. He promised us redemption and salvation. He gave His only son to die for our salvation, for our eternity. This life is just a doorway into the next life, the forever life, where sickness, infirmities, disabilities, and sin do not exist." Wow! That's it, she thinks. In that moment, her perspective begins to shift, ever so slightly; it is starting to make sense in some odd way.

"God wants you to know that he has a ministry for you to walk into but the doubt, feelings of abandonment, and disappointment are blocking you from the freedom God has for you," the man said.

Lori begins to cry; she can't stop the tears flowing down her face. She is overcome by a presence, a feeling that is indescribable. It is like she has been in darkness for years and someone has opened the curtains to let the light in. She realizes that she has been praying for God to heal Tommy, and her unmet expectations and disappointment have kept her angry and bitter. She realizes that she has been expecting something from God that He never promised.

She has been expecting something different in life that she was not going to get. She has been chasing "normal" and is angry because she has experienced one let down after another. She has been so angry and sad about what she did not have, about what Tommy did not have, that she failed to appreciate all that they did have.

Somewhere along the way, she stopped seeing the beauty of grace and salvation. She did not see all the wonderful things about Tommy, about their life. They didn't have "normal", but it really isn't so bad, she thinks. In the big picture of eternity, it really isn't so bad at all. She felt as though she has been the one who has been in darkness, not Tommy. She begins to openly weep. Somewhere through her tears, she hears the man ask, "If this person is you, stand to your feet so we can pray for you."

Lori was already on her feet. The next thing she knew, she was surrounded by complete strangers all praying for her, some gently embracing her, others praying out loud. She could not contain the well of emotions flowing out of her. It felt like the weight of a thousand pounds being lifted from her.

She realizes she has been angry at life and God because her expectations were not being met. She wasn't going to love God fully or trust him fully because she didn't have what she thought she deserved. She didn't have what she thought Tommy deserved. Her relationship and view of God has been based on a condition. Her conditions were: I'll trust you if you heal my son, I'll trust you if there is no suffering, and I'll trust you if you keep me happy and free from any difficulties. Her expectations have been unrealistic, maybe even unfair and selfish.

She has been so focused on what God has not given her or what He has not done that she failed to see what He has done. She has been missing the big picture, she thinks. The disappointment and bitterness clouded her perspective of what life is really about, the hope of life. She has gained a new perspective that highlights hope.

She can see plainly now that she has been lining Tommy up side by side to all the things this world values. But what about God, what about the life after this one, what is valuable there? When Tommy dies or when I die, she thinks, will it matter if he was married, went to college, drove a car, had children, and so on? No, she concludes. None of that will matter. What will matter, she ponders?

When she compares Tommy's abilities with eternal values, he is on target. Every milestone reached. His faith is childlike, he is honest, he loves, he is forgiving, he doesn't judge others, he doesn't see color, status, or any diversity that bogs the rest of us down. None of it matters to him. He doesn't question God. He simply believes. She can't even begin to fathom the freedom and joy she is feeling.

God didn't do this to Tommy. God did not give Tommy autism. God didn't do this to me. God hasn't abandoned me. In fact, He has walked with me all along. He was with us at the meeting with the judge, the evaluator, the specialist, the prom, leading us back to church, leading me here, she thinks as she wipes the tears running down her cheek.

She starts thinking about "normal" and how long she has been chasing it for Tommy. It has felt like she could never quite get there, as if stuck on some invisible treadmill. She has been chasing the wrong thing. She whispers a prayer to God, "Please forgive me and teach me how to love the life we have, to love our normal." She decides she will seek God and focus on what matters, trusting that God will help her through and give her the joy she feels flooding her heart tonight, in this moment.

She finally returns to find Tommy talking to one of the kids beside him. She looks at his face, and for the first time in a long time, she doesn't see losses. She sees his happiness. She sees the world through his eyes, not the eyes of loss viewed through her own eyes for so long. He is smiling, loved, happy, and content. She hugs him tightly and tells him how much she loves him.

As the bus pulls away from the hotel, Lori is ready for the next phase of her life. She can't wait to share her experience with Robert. She is ready to get off the treadmill and relieved she has finally learned how to let go of what was lost. No more chasing "normal", at least the one she expected. She will start enjoying the normal she already has and plan a future around the things that matter.

As she stares out the window on the long ride home, she knows things will not be perfect and this will not cure Tommy from autism, but she believes it has healed her. It has corrected her vision, made it clearer, and changed her perspective, in the ways that count. She thinks about how much she has grown in a weekend. Thank you God, she whispers.

Her heart is full of gratitude and love. If she grew this much in a weekend, she wonders what life will bring in her older years. Older years, that thought is surely one she avoids. It immediately causes her heart to skip a beat, wondering who will take care of Tommy when she is gone. God help me find peace when I am facing the unknown, she prays silently. What does our future hold...?

We have to change our perspective of our reality to move to a place of healthier adapting. It is pivotal to getting of the treadmill of grief. Spending hours on a treadmill is not my idea of a good time. However, trying to reach the ever elusive "normal" in our society is like being stuck on an eternal treadmill. You are running as fast as you can only to stumble on yet another unmet milestone or challenge that trips you up.

Lori's view shifted through a spiritual experience with God. Her perspective of life and what was important changed drastically, therefore changing her view of their condition or station in life. Learning how to accept the differences and challenges created by the disability is one thing. Learning how to adapt to those differences in a way that makes room for joy and peace in you and your family's lives is the key to getting off the treadmill.

I personally can identify with Lori because my faith has certainly helped me gain a better view of what is important for both me and my son. Healthy adapting means you stop chasing or longing for what has been lost and start focusing on what matters most to you. If you are not a spiritual person, you can still redefine what is important in your life.

Our kids may never meet society's definition of "normal", but so what! It doesn't mean that we don't have a normal because we do. It also doesn't mean that our normal is any less valuable than the expected "normal".

We never give up on helping our kids reach their full potential. But if the dream of the expected "normal" is always what we compare them to, then we will become stuck in unending cycles of grief, hoping for an outcome that does not arrive.

We all know the definition of insanity is "doing the same thing over and over expecting different results." Wishing for "normal" or looking for an end to our grief will leave us in limbo! Even people functioning close to "normal" still have moments of grief when they find themselves on the outside.

The most powerful tool in adapting is learning how to appreciate, value, and expect our own individualized normal in the context of the disability. Our children do not have to meet all, part, or any of our societies expected norms to have a happy life, full of quality and joy.

Emily Perl Kingsley expressed this picture beautifully in her story of Holland. Below is an insert of her story.

Welcome to Holland
  By Emily Perl Kingsley
  C1987 by Emily Perl Kingsley. All rights reserved

I am often asked to describe the experience of raising a child with a disability – to try to help people who have not shared that unique experience to understand it, to imagine how it would feel. It's like this.....
When you're going to have a baby, it's like planning a fabulous vacation trip – to Italy. You buy a bunch of guide books and make your wonderful plans. The Coliseum. The Michelangelo David. The gondolas in Venice. You many learn some handy phrases in Italian. It's all very exciting.
After months of eager anticipation, the day finally arrives. You pack your bags and off you go. Several hours later, the plane lands. The stewardess comes in and says, "Welcome to Holland."
"Holland?!?" you say. "What do you mean Holland?? I signed up for Italy! I'm supposed to be in Italy. All my life I've dreamed of going to Italy."
But there's been a change in the flight plan. They've landed in Holland and there you must stay.
The important thing is that they haven't taken you to a horrible, disgusting, filthy place, full of pestilence, famine and disease. It's just a different place.

*So you must go out and buy new guide books. And you
must learn a whole new language. And you will meet a
whole new group of people you would have never met.
It's just a different place. Its slower-placed than Italy,
less flashy than Italy. But after you've been there for a
while and you catch your breath, you look around... and
you begin to notice that Holland has windmills....and
Holland has tulips. Holland even has Rembrandts.
But everyone you know is busy coming and going from
Italy... and they're all bragging about what a wonderful
time they had there. And for the rest of your life, you will
say "Yes, that's where I was supposed to go. That's what
I had planned."
And the pain of that will never, ever, ever, go
away....because the loss of that dream is a very very
significant loss.
But... if you spend your life mourning the fact that you
didn't get to Italy, you may never be free to enjoy the very
special, the very lovely things... about Holland.*

She describes the loss of "normal" by using the analogy
of Italy versus Holland. In her example, she paints a picture of
being in Holland, yet surrounded by people who are all going to
Italy. She is expressing the loss of "normal" when living in a
society that boasts about "normal". It is a real loss that causes
real pain, but if we spend our lives in mourning, we will not be
able to appreciate our lives outside the "normal" limits.

We love and celebrate our children! I am sure you could
spend hours telling me all about what makes your child special
and amazing. And you would be right. Our kids are amazing! I
believe every individual born is significant and valuable.

Lori's life-changing experience drastically altered her
perspective on what mattered. I am a firm believer that
perception largely shapes reality. If we perceive that our lives are
good, we will feel good about our station in life, even if it is
different than we expected. If we perceive our situations as less
than, it will leave us dissatisfied.

It is the comparison to "normal" that can shape our

164

perceptions as less than. It is also the world's perception of "normal" that shapes attitudes and prejudices.

At one of my speaking engagements where I was presenting the A-typical Cyclic Grief model, I was listening to one of the other presenters ahead of me. This speaker was encouraging parents and sharing stories of triumph and hope. As I was listening to this amazing story of a young man who beat the odds and graduated from high school with a diploma, I realized the miracles being touted were not possibilities for my son. The speaker was bragging about how he is now employed full time, renting his own apartment, and looking at a future of complete independence. Wow!

He went on to encourage parents by saying, "This young man is going on leading a "normal" life. You just never know. Maybe your child will too, so never give up." As I listened to him talk, I glanced over at a couple sitting at my table; they had their child with them. She was profoundly intellectually challenged and completely paralyzed.

Their child was in a wheelchair and dependent on her parents for everything. Bathing, feeding, and toileting were their daily norms. She could not speak or do much of anything for herself. I felt my eyes fill with tears as I realized that this message of hope would not be theirs to claim, ever.

They were politely listening as the story of success was painted. It occurred to me that day, even in the circles of disability, the gold standard is to achieve "normal" or close to "normal." So what happens if "normal" is not a possibility? All hope is lost? These parents have no hope? It's as if "normal" equals success and outside of "normal" or below "normal" equals defeat. I don't believe that, but the message sure emphasized it, at least to my ears. I am sure the speaker's only aim was to encourage parents and it was an amazing story but...

The point is, neither you nor your child has to achieve normal functioning to have success. "Normal" does not equal happiness or quality of life. Honestly, the love, dedication, pride, joy, and compassion I observed in those parents for their child showed a true picture of success!

To love when it requires more than expected for longer

than expected without reward or repayment is a love that goes beyond anything this world can measure. They had their own normal, and it appeared, at least from the outside, that they had learned to make it good! Their daughter was precious. She had been loved well! She touched my life that day in a powerful way and never knew it!

Everyone's situation is going to be slightly different. We have to learn to think "outside the "normal" box." Learn to enjoy "Holland." Changing your perspective will not eliminate feelings of grief or loss altogether, nor will it change the disability. However, ending the constant comparisons to "normal", learning to anticipate milestones, and focusing on what you decide is important, not what society decides, will get you on your way to healthier adapting.

Challenge Questions:
1. How do you define normal?

2. How do you think society defines "normal"?

3. What is a day in your life like?

4. Have you been chasing "normal"? Do you feel like you have been stuck on a treadmill, always trying to figure out how to get closer to the mark?

5. List the top 5 things you feel are most important in life.

6. Are those 5 things tied to "normal"?

7. How would you describe quality of life?

8. What do you currently need to achieve that quality?

Remember: It is not our circumstance but rather our perception of the circumstance that determines our emotional reactions. We think, feel, and act on these perceptions.

Chapter 16: Life Outside the "Normal" Limits: The Final Frontier.

The loud crash jolts her from a sound sleep. She sleeps on and off most days since she turned seventy-five years old. She laughingly refers to them as cat naps. She hears her home health caregiver, Joan, coming through the door. Sorry Ms. Jones, she says. I didn't mean to knock over the planter but my purse got hung and jerked it over. Lori tells her its fine. She didn't like that plant to begin with. She was given the plant when Robert passed away and it's a reminder of that dreadful day.

She remembers how peacefully he passed and longs for the day to be reunited with him, except for Tommy. Tommy is soon to be fifty and such a kind man. He has grown in his relationship with all of his brothers and sisters over the years. Scott and Ella both agree and want Tommy to come live with them when Lori is gone. They have always been closest, because they live in the same town, and they see them regularly. She recalls the agonizing years of not knowing who would take care of Tommy and lived in constant fear of dying, not the fear of death, but the fear of Tommy's loss. She is so comforted to know he will be with Scott and Ella.

Her mind drifts back over the years as it does often these days. Her time is growing short; the cancer is untreatable. Tommy doesn't know yet. She wants him to enjoy the time they have together without the constant worry. She plans to tell him in the final days. Maybe soon, she thinks.

She remembers the birth of their first grandchild, Jackson. Ella was so beautiful, even pregnant. She invited Lori to come into the birth of her second child, but the baby was breech, so it was not allowed. The invitation meant so much to Lori; words could never describe the depth of her gratitude to Ella.

James and Pam married soon after graduating college. Pam went on to medical school and James became a teacher. They had several children together blessing her and Robert with a number of grandchildren they enjoyed immensely through the years.

Carrie built a successful career and enjoyed a life filled

with travel and entertainment. Robert had been so proud of all of his children. He never referred to Tommy as his stepson and Tommy called him dad from the age of ten years old. Robert was Tommy's dad, she thinks. Tommy was so young when Mike attempted suicide. Tommy barely knew him and never saw him again after the incident. Robert raised him. He won Robert's heart from the beginning. She could not have asked for a better father for sweet Tommy.

Tommy matured, eventually getting his driver's license in his early twenties and enjoying some level of independence, going to visit his grandparents on weekends. They lived in the country, so he could make the drive easily. He took on household chores to earn money and worked for Lori part-time in her office. He enjoyed saying he had a job, so it was hard for him when she retired, but she convinced him lots of people take early retirement. So, that is what he did. The memory makes her smile.

She thinks back to the day she opened her office. It was her dream to have her own place so Tommy could work at least one afternoon a week. She finished graduate school and got her license for professional counseling. She still can't believe how all of it came together.

She remembers her years of unending grief that led to the development of a grief model to help other parents understand their own feelings and not feel isolated like she and many others had to experience. She believed, even though she had made peace and learned to adapt, there would be many parents who came after her that would need help. It really became her passion. She believed it was the ministry that preacher talked about on that night when her perspective was changed.

She loved speaking engagements, and even more, she loved talking with parents at the end. She was always so overjoyed when they would share how much the information helped them. Tommy would often travel with her and so did Robert in his retirement years. Robert was her biggest supporter. He would often talk with other parents as well and enjoyed it immensely.

She eventually wrote and published a book to talk about

the grief experience that parents share when they have to live a life outside of "normal". She would openly tell people about her experience with God and her healing on that night. She believes the book is a direct outflow from her perspective change and her relationship with God. She is so thankful for all that God has done in her life and through her life to help others, to help her, and to help Tommy.

She reflects back to Mike's suicide attempt and the agony of those years. She remembers specifically hearing the strange message on the radio station about shattered lives feeding the multitudes. She didn't even know five people back then, much less a multitude, yet God somehow impressed on her that her shattered life would be used in some way to help people. Funny, she muses. Looking back on that now, it all makes sense.

She thinks about all the years of learning how to not let her circumstances dictate her views on life. Her mantra became, "If you can't change the circumstance, you can change how you view the circumstance." Finding joy and happiness within the circumstance was the key.

It took some time combined with trial and error to figure out what all they needed to take care of Tommy and have quality time together, as a couple, and as a family. Tommy didn't move out of the house like typical kids do at a certain age. They did not ever have years together when all the kids had flown the coop. But they had a good life, nonetheless, she reflects.

They hired caregivers at times to stay with Tommy, so they could have some vacations together, just the two of them. Other times, they took Tommy with them so he could enjoy vacations.

They learned how to have a more adult type relationship with Tommy as best they could. They built him an apartment downstairs to give him some independence. He was able to fully take care of himself with the exception of cooking and managing money.

He loved becoming an uncle and enjoyed the size of the family as we grew, she recalls with a smile. He finally felt a part, not left out. Lori's perspective remained mostly healthy over the years. She remained focused on Tommy being happy and having some quality of life, rather than the life everyone expects to have.

Joan's hand startles her back to the here and now. "Ms. Jones, she says, would you like some hot tea?" "No thank you," Lori replies. Joan is a kind woman and Lori is thankful to have someone as nice as she for her caregiver.

She hears the back door open and in hops Jackson her eldest grandson. He is now twenty-six and has a girlfriend he seems pretty smitten by. Jackson belts out, "Hey Nonna, I just wanted to stop by to share some good news." Here it comes, she thinks. "I'm getting married," he exclaims! No surprise there, she muses. "Congratulations Jackson," she tells him as she gives him a big hug. "Your papa would be so proud."

Tommy walked up excited to see his nephew. Jackson gave him a high five and a big hug. He talked to Tommy for a few minutes, and then said he couldn't stay long. He had to be somewhere. Lori is so blessed to have her family, she thinks. She remembers when she and Robert first married, when it felt like his family. Now it just feels like their family, her family, Tommy's family. Oh how she misses Robert. I love you, she whispers hoping somehow he can hear her.

Joan reaches over to cover her with a blanket, as she feels herself drifting off to sleep again. Tommy kisses her on the forehead, telling her to rest. She squeezes his hand and whispers, "I love you son." He whispers back, "I love you too, mom."

Let's go ahead and answer the question you may have pondered a few times. Are you Lori? Let me just say that parts of Lori's story mirrors my own life story, but only in parts. Which parts you ask? I'll leave you guessing on that one. Obviously, I am not deceased nor is my husband. The fictional characters used in the writing of this book were created and designed specifically to protect the privacy of others. Let's go back to Lori.

Lori talks about her fears when she didn't know who would take care of Tommy when she died. If we are being honest, it is a fear many of us face. It is not a pleasant topic to discuss. In fact, grief is not easy to talk about, but necessary to confront and walk through.

Sometimes there are no clear answers to some of the questions. Particularly, the questions of life after both parents are gone. If you fall into that category, you are not alone.

I find myself faced with those same fears. I remind myself that life has a way of changing and maybe there is not an answer today but one will emerge later. As the numbers of children identified with a developmental disability grow, it will mandate the need for more states to open long-term care facilities. At least that is my hope. There are also special needs trusts attorneys and other life planning specialist that can help us with future planning options for life after we are gone. I strongly recommend every parent to educate yourself about options regardless of your financial position. Even if you don't have all the answers or resources you will at least have information about what is available.

We are also faced with the loss of typical retirement years. Our years of care-giving for our children don't stop around the age of eighteen, they continue for the rest of our lives for many of us. If we as parents do not figure out how to adapt and plan for those adjustments, we run the risk of becoming bitter and resentful, with poor quality of life in the future.

Think about how your life is impacted by your child's disability. We as parents should consider our own needs, expectations, and goals as well as our child's. We have to consider the limitations of our child/children. What resources will be required to get our needs met as we travel through life?

Perhaps developing a sort of "family needs plan" would jumpstart your thoughts about your future. Develop a plan that would help you answer question to identify specific goals and needs. For example, do you want to travel in retirement; do you have people identified to take care of your child; are there funds set aside to help with the care; what about vacations, couple time, etc?

Post high school years can be problematic as well. Many parents struggle with finding placements for their child once they turn twenty-one and can no longer stay in the school system. Start searching your local area for resources. Find out what is out there for your child in adult years. There are supplementary programs that may help subsidize funding for care during the day, so you can work if need be.

Although it may be a loose script or plan, it may help to reduce the fear of the unknown. It may also help to lessen the emotional impacts of future losses. Awareness can be a powerful tool. Talk openly about how the disability affects the long range plan for the entire family.

The family plan needs to include quality of life in the here and now as well. This is a long haul for many of us. A close friend, who also has a child with a developmental disability, used to tell me, "This is not a sprint, it is a marathon and we need to run it like a marathon." We are in it for the duration. Remember, we have to put our oxygen mask on first.

Finding peace and quality of life in the midst of your circumstance is absolutely critical to healthy adapting. I encourage you to sit down with your partner, or alone if you are single, to think through your needs and how to make adjustments to help you sustain balance and better quality of life.

In conclusion, A-typical Cyclic Grief is a common and shared reaction to raising a child with a disability that places them and you outside of "normal". Understanding the grief process and working through the challenging emotions will help you adapt in healthier ways.

Remember, Lori went through phases of denial, anger, guilt, emotional conflict, isolation, depression, renewed sense of hope, and unmet milestones many times over. This is common with ACG. As long as she continued to chase "normal", tripping over unmet expectations along the way, she continued to be stuck in the yoyo effect of ACG. Breaking the repetitive cycles of grief **takes** a mind shift. Letting go of the "normal" that was lost and creating a new normal, embracing the normal you have been given, occurs **when** a mind shift takes place.

Making changes in your life to keep your marriage and family in balance will help you sustain the additional challenges. Talking openly about your feelings and your experiences stops the isolation and opens doorways for the support you need.

Having a better understanding of why you feel the way you do takes the shame out of your grief. Nothing will prevent you from experiencing some level of grief when "normal" is lost, but we can break the cycles that keep us stuck.

Learn to recognize the grief in yourself and in your spouse or partner when it comes. Give yourself permission to grieve and talk about your feelings when they occur. Explore what thoughts are behind the grief. Is it the comparison to "normal", secondary trauma from something someone said; self-imposed guilt; depression; fatigue; or an unmet milestone? If you are unable to talk with a partner, find a friend that understands and has experienced ACG for support.

We can be aware of milestones coming in the future and what they may represent. We can think about our later years and who will care for our children if need be and how we will manage the retirement years.

Just remember, traveling through the stages of grief surrounding the loss of "normal" is a common experience shared by many. Grieving in silence without support from others leads to unhealthy outcomes. We do NOT have to struggle in silence! There is hope and emotional healing for a brighter future.

We love and celebrate our children. They are NOT our source of grief. Nonetheless, we grieve! Let's not spend our whole lives stuck on a treadmill grieving in silence!

I would much rather spend my time enjoying my son and my life as it is instead of trying to make it something different or wishing it was different. Enjoy your child/children and your family. There is so much beauty on this road less traveled.

We have the unique privilege to see things from a whole new vantage point. It may not be what we expected or what the majority has but if we can learn to see the value in what we have it will change our perspectives. Yes there are losses and there are also gains. Face the losses and work through the grief then enjoy the beauty. Take some time to think through the following questions on the next page.

Challenge Questions:

1. How do you envision your later years?

2. What about retirement? Do you want to travel?

3. Do you have a special needs trust/will or plan for life after you are gone?

4. Who will care for your child? If you don't know, don't panic. It is common for people to not know the answer to that question just yet. Keep it at the forefront, though; stay aware of resources in your community.

5. What about now? Do you have time away from your child? Time with friends or simply to sleep on the couch all day, both can help recharge your battery.

6. Do you have other children? Have you talked as a family about future years or the present?

Remember: Letting go of the expected "normal" is the pathway to developing your new normal. You may not know all the answers but you can think about possibilities and resources.

Works Cited

Bruce, E. & Schultz, C. (2002). Non-finite loss and challenges to communication between parents and professionals. *British Journal of Special Education, 29*, 9-13.

Luterman, D. (2004). Counseling families of children with hearing loss and special needs. *Volta Review, 104(4)*, 215-220.

Teel, C.S. (1991). Chronic sorrow: analysis of the concept. *Journal of Advanced Nursing, Volume 16, Issue 11*, 1267–1393.

WELCOME TO HOLLAND by Emily Perl Kingsley. c1987 All rights reserved. Retrieved from the web: 04/03/2017. Permission to reprint granted by the author.

Resources & References

On Death and Dying: Elisabeth Kübler-Ross: Originally published: 1969. This book introduced the five stages of grief in response to death. The stages are denial, anger, bargaining, depression, and acceptance.

The Sneeches and Other Stories by Dr. Seuss: published 1953.

Centers for Disease Control and Prevention | USA.gov *https://www.usa.gov/federal-agencies/centers-for-disease-control-and-prevention: Retrieved from the web on 10/2016*

U.S. News & World Report: News, Rankings and Analysis on Politics *https://www.usnews.com/: Retrieved from the web on 08/2016*

Resources & References

Dictionary: Merriam-Webster
  https://www.merriam-webster.com/ Web Retrieval 06/2010

National Suicide Prevention Lifeline
  Call 1-800-273-8255
  Available 24 hours every day.
  https://suicidepreventionlifeline.org/:
  Web Retrieval 04/2017

Rudolph the Red-Nosed Reindeer (TV Movie 1964) - IMDb Story of the misfit toys.

Rain Man (Movie 1988) - IMDb Movie portraying an autistic man.

Pocahontas (Movie 1995) - IMDb Disney movie featuring the character Kocoum.

Artist: Kenny Rogers Album: The Gambler Released: 1978 Genre: Pop.

9 781974 060443